BEST *of* ARIZONA

CHEF'S RECIPES
FROM ARIZONA'S FAVORITE
RESORTS & RESTAURANTS

BY

MARJORIE SCAFFIDI

DESIGN & PRODUCTION
KIMURA/BINGHAM DESIGN

TREASURE CHEST PUBLICATIONS

ACKNOWLEDGEMENTS:

This book was truly a group effort. My special thanks to Mary Scaffidi, Jim Allen, Julia Meeks, Sara Minkoff, Andy Rakoczy, Sally Sommer, Bill Weiland,C.E.C. and the chefs and restaurants who contributed such wonderful recipes.

— Marjorie Scaffidi

TABLE OF CONTENTS

HOW TO
USE THIS BOOK

To give you a quick estimate of the time and techniques involved in preparing recipes, summary statements are included in each recipe. The times listed represent the total time for each corresponding section.

For unusual ingredients, descriptions and substitution suggestions are listed with each recipe. However, if the ingredient appears in several recipes, you can find explanations in the ingredient substitution chart on page 286.

APPETIZERS

Scallop Ceviche

Crab Nachos

Fried Avocados

Stuffed Mushrooms

Shrimp DeJonghe

Mussels in White Wine

Deviled Eggs Romanoff

Prickly Pear Margarita

Gnocchi Verde

Roasted Anaheim Chilies Stuffed with
  a Chevre & Toasted Walnut Mousse

Marinated Salmon with Dill Sauce

Salmon Grave Lox with Fresh Dill Cream

Softshell Crab and Crabcake Appetizer

Michael's Salsa with Tortilla Chips

For more appetizers, please see index

SCALLOP CEVICHE

1/2 lb. Bay Scallops
Juice of 1 Lime
Juice of 1 Lemon
1/4 small Red Onion, minced fine
1 small Plum Tomato, diced
1 Green Onion, chopped
1 small Jalapeño, minced fine
1 small Serrano Chile, minced fine
1 bunch Cilantro, chopped
1t Ketchup
1/2t Rice Wine Vinegar
1/2t Grand Marnier
1 pinch Cayenne Pepper
1 pinch ground Black Pepper
Salt, to taste

Mix well and refrigerate overnight.

Serves 4

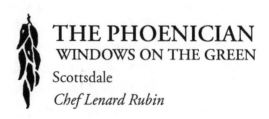

THE PHOENICIAN
WINDOWS ON THE GREEN
Scottsdale
Chef Lenard Rubin

CRAB NACHOS

3 Corn Tortillas, 6-inch diameter
3T Sour Cream
4 oz. Crabmeat
1C Monterey Jack, shredded
1C Cheddar Cheese, shredded
1 Jalapeño, cut into 12 rings
Guacamole

Deep fry:
Deep fry the tortillas. Drain and set on paper towels to absorb any excess oil.

Broil few minutes:
Set the tortillas on a baking dish or pan. Mix the cheeses in a bowl. Spoon the sour cream, crabmeat, and cheese on the tortillas. Broil until the cheese melts.

Serve:
Using a pizza cutter, cut each tortilla into 4 pieces. Arrange the nachos around guacamole on a serving platter. Top each nacho with a jalapeño ring.

Serves 4

JOHN JACOB'S
EL PARADOR
Tucson
Chef Daniel Jacob

FRIED AVOCADOS

1 bottle Mexican Beer
3C Flour
1/2C Cilantro, chopped
Salt and Cayenne Pepper, to taste
Sprinkling of flour
2 Avocados, cut in quarters

Garnish:
Prickly Pear Cactus Jelly or Barbeque Sauce

Coat:
Pour the beer into a mixing bowl. Add 3C flour gradually, until the mixture has the consistency of thick pancake batter. Mix in the cilantro, salt, and cayenne pepper. Sprinkle flour on a plate. Dip the avocados in the flour, and then in the beer batter.

Deep fry 3 minutes:
Fry the avocados in oil until they are crispy. When done, place them on paper towels to absorb the oil.

Serve:
Serve with prickly pear cactus jelly or barbecue sauce.

Serves 2

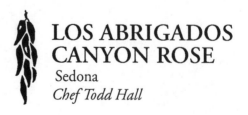

**LOS ABRIGADOS
CANYON ROSE**
Sedona
Chef Todd Hall

STUFFED MUSHROOMS

4 oz. Butter
1 Onion, minced
1t fresh Garlic, chopped
2 lbs. Mushrooms, minced
1-1/2C Breadcrumbs
1C Romano Cheese, freshly grated
Salt and Pepper, to taste
30 to 50 large Mushroom Caps
Sprinkling of Seasoned Breadcrumbs
Romano Cheese, freshly grated
Melted Butter, to taste

Saute few minutes:
Saute the onion, garlic, and mushrooms in butter. Add 1-1/2C breadcrumbs, 1C cheese, salt, and pepper. Cool.

Fill and coat:
Spoon the onion mixture into the mushroom caps. Top with a sprinkling of breadcrumbs, cheese, and melted butter. Add the ingredients in the order given. Use just enough to cover the mushrooms.

Bake 10 minutes:
Bake at 450 degrees.

Serves 8 to 10

SCORDATO'S
RESTAURANT
Tucson
Chef Jim Scordato

SHRIMP DE JONGHE

16 small-medium Shrimp, peeled and deveined
8T Butter
1t Lemon Juice
Salt and Pepper, to taste
1/8t Garlic Powder
4T Bread Crumbs
1/8t dried Parsley

This recipe is rich and delicious. For a
lighter version, use less butter.

Saute few minutes:
Saute the shrimp in butter 2 to 3 minutes, until the shrimp have
just turned white. Add the lemon juice, salt, pepper, and garlic
powder and heat for a moment.

Bake 5 minutes:
Place the shrimp mixture in a casserole. Sprinkle bread crumbs
and parsley on top, and bake at 375 degrees.

Serves 2

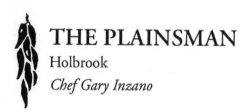

THE PLAINSMAN
Holbrook
Chef Gary Inzano

MUSSELS
IN WHITE WINE

3T Butter
1 medium Onion, thinly sliced
3 cloves Garlic, minced
1-1/2C dry White Wine
2 Bay Leaves
2-1/2 to 3 lbs. Mussels, cleaned and beards removed

Garnish:
Chopped Parsley
Lemon Wedges

Saute and boil 8 to 12 minutes:
In a large saucepan, saute the onion and garlic in butter until
tender but not brown. Add the wine and bay leaves and boil 2 to 4
minutes. Add the mussels, cover, and cook 3 to 5 minutes or until
the mussels open. Discard any unopened mussels.

Serve:
Pour the mussels and sauce into serving bowls. Sprinkle with
chopped parsley and serve immediately with lemon wedges.

Serves 6

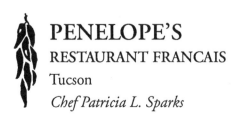

PENELOPE'S
RESTAURANT FRANCAIS
Tucson
Chef Patricia L. Sparks

DEVILED EGGS ROMANOFF

12 Eggs
1/4C Mayonnaise
1t Anchovy Paste
2T Butter
1/2t English Mustard*
1/4t Worcestershire Sauce
Pinch of White Pepper
Pinch of Salt

Garnish:
1T Fresh Black or Red Caviar
Fresh Parsley

*English mustard is a coarse, stone ground
mustard. If not available, try Dijon.

Hard boil:
Hard boil the eggs. When done, immerse the eggs in cold water.
Cooled eggs are easier to peel. Peel and cut each egg in half
lengthwise. Carefully remove the yolks and place them a mixing bowl.
Set the whites aside.

Blend:
Place the egg yolks, mayonnaise, anchovy paste, butter, mustard,
Worcestershire sauce, white pepper, and salt in a blender. Blend until
smooth. Correct the seasonings to taste.

Fill and garnish:
Fill the egg whites with the yolk mixture by using a spoon or piping
sack. Garnish each egg with a pinch of caviar and decorate the point
of each egg with a sprig of
parsley. Arrange on a tray.

Chill.

Serves 12

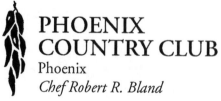

**PHOENIX
COUNTRY CLUB**
Phoenix
Chef Robert R. Bland

PRICKLY PEAR MARGARITA

1-1/2T Sweet and Sour Mix
1-1/2T Prickly Pear Syrup*
1T Triple Sec
3T Tequila
1/2T Lime Juice

Garnish:
Red Pepper
Tumbleweed shoot

*Prickly pear is a cactus. Prickly pear products
can be found in gourmet and southwest gift shops.

Mix:
Shake all the ingredients together. Pour over ice, or blend with ice.

Serve:
Serve the margarita in a salt-rimmed glass, garnished with red
pepper and tumbleweed shoot.

Serves 1

JANOS
Tucson
Chef Janos Wilder

GNOCCHI VERDE

1/4 lb. Butter
1 lb. fresh Spinach, chopped*
1 lb. Ricotta Cheese
1/4C imported grated Parmesan Cheese
Salt and freshly ground Pepper, to taste
Alfredo Sauce, recipe follows

*If you use frozen spinach, squeeze and strain
excess water.

Saute few minutes:
Saute the spinach and butter over medium heat. Cook until the
spinach wilts. Add the cheeses, salt, and pepper. Fold until
blended.

Chill:
It will be easier to form the gnocchi when the cheese and spinach
are cold.

Form gnocchi:
Roll the spinach mixture into balls 2 inches in diameter. Place 2
to 3 balls in each of 4 baking dishes.

Bake 15 minutes:
Bake at 350 degrees.

Serve:
Serve with Alfredo Sauce.

Serves 4

ALFREDO SAUCE

1/4C Shallots, chopped
1/4C Brandy
1 pint Heavy Cream
1/4C grated Parmesan Cheese
1/4t White Pepper
Sprinkle of Salt
1/4C Water
Cornstarch as required to thicken (approx.1/4C)

Saute and simmer 18 to 20 minutes:
Heat the shallots in a saucepan until they wilt. Add the brandy and simmer 1 to 2 minutes. Add the cream, cheese, pepper, and salt. Simmer slowly for 10 to 15 minutes. Mix the cornstarch with water. Slowly stir into the pan until the sauce is thick enough to coat the back of a spoon.

HASSAYAMPA INN
Prescott
Chef Linda Rose

ROASTED ANAHEIM CHILIES STUFFED WITH A CHEVRE AND TOASTED WALNUT MOUSSE

6 Anaheim Chilies
3C Walnuts, chopped
8 oz. Chevre, room temperature*
Salt, to taste
Pepper, to taste
Tabasco Sauce, to taste
Worchestershire Sauce, to taste
Fresh Plum Chutney, recipe follows

*Chevre is peppered goat cheese. To substitute,
use feta cheese topped with freshly ground pepper.

Prepare the chilies:
Roast, peel, and deseed the chilies. The appendix describes how
to peel chilies. (Use the "deep fry until skins turn brown"
method.) To deseed, make a small incision at the top of the
chilies, near their stems, and carefully remove the seeds. Do not
cut through the chilies. If desired, an artful "X" can be seared
onto the peeled chilies by pressing them against a hot grill. The
"X" is for presentation only.

Prepare the filling:
Bake the walnuts in a 300 degree oven 6 to 8 minutes until they
become toasted. Turn the walnuts frequently while toasting to
avoid scorching. Mix the toasted walnuts with cheese, salt,
pepper, Tabasco sauce, and Worchestershire sauce.

Stuffing:
Using a pastry bag with a tube tip, squeeze the cheese mixture into the chile openings.
Chill.

Serve:
Slice the chilies and serve garnished with Fresh Plum Chutney.

Serves 6

FRESH PLUM CHUTNEY

1/2C Sugar
1/2C Vinegar
6 fresh Plums, diced
2T Ginger
2 Jalapeño Peppers, diced
1 Onion, diced
1 small bunch Cilantro

Simmer 15 minutes:
Heat the sugar with a few drops of water over high heat. Mix and cook until lightly brown. Reduce the heat to medium, and add the vinegar, 3 plums, ginger, and peppers. Cook until the mixture turns to a syrup. Let cool.

Puree:
Puree the pepper mixture, onion, cilantro, and 3 plums.

HYATT REGENCY
SCOTTSDALE
AT GAINEY RANCH
GOLDEN SWAN

Scottsdale
Chef Anton Brunbauer

MARINATED SALMON WITH DILL SAUCE

Served on rye bread with a little sweet butter, some caviar, and a glass of champagne, this salmon is a magnificent summer appetizer!

3 lbs. Salmon, center cut
2T Sugar
4t White Pepper, freshly crushed
2T Kosher salt
4 bunches fresh Dillweed stalks
3 Egg Yolks
3T Imported Dijon Mustard
Freshly ground Black Pepper, to taste
1C Vegetable Oil
1/2t Sugar
Juice of 1/2 Lemon
2T snipped fresh Dill

Garnish:
Boston Lettuce
3 hollowed Lemon Cups
6 Scallion Shoots, trimmed
1 sprig fresh Dill
Freshly ground Pepper

Preparation:
Fillet the salmon, leaving the skin on. Be sure to remove any small bones with a tweezer. Pat the fish dry. You will end up with two filets.

Mix 2T sugar, white pepper, and salt in a bowl.

Bruise the dillweed stalks by pounding lightly with the side of a mallet. Bruising releases more flavor from the herb.

Coat:
Sprinkle a large, shallow dish with 1/3 of the sugar mixture. Place one of the salmon filets, skin side down over the mixture. Spread the

pounded dill stalks on the salmon. Sprinkle with another 1/3 sugar mixture. Lay the remaining salmon filet, skin side up, on top of the first filet and sugar. Sprinkle with the remaining 1/3 sugar mixture. Set a plate on the salmon, but do not weight it. Cover with foil or plastic to create an airtight seal.

Refrigerate 3 days:
Turn the salmon each day and baste with juices that accumulate. You are curing the salmon. After 3 days, not only will it be fresh, but the marinade flavors will have spread throughout the fish.

When done, wipe most of the marinade from the salmon. Reserve 3 dill sprigs and 2T marinade juices. Chop the reserved dill, and strain the reserved marinade. Slice the salmon into thin slices at a diagonal as you would smoked salmon.

Mix the sauce:
In a mixing bowl, beat the egg yolks, mustard, and black pepper. Gradually beat the oil into the egg and mustard mixture in a slow, steady stream. Whisk constantly until it becomes smooth and thick. Stir in the reserved dill, reserved marinade, 1/2t sugar, lemon juice, and snipped dill. Save the hollowed lemon for the garnish.

Garnish:
Line a serving platter with Boston lettuce leaves. Arrange the salmon slices so they overlap like a fan on one side of the plate. Cut three lemons in half and remove the fruit. Fill the hollowed lemon cups with sauce and scallion shoots. Arrange the cups on the platter. Finish with a sprig of fresh dill, and sprinkle with freshly ground pepper.

Serves 6

EL TOVAR
Grand Canyon
Chef Esteban Colon

SALMON GRAVE LOX WITH FRESH DILL CREAM

1C Kosher Salt
2C Light Brown Sugar
1/2C fresh Dill, chopped
1/2C fresh Fennel root, chopped
8 Bay Leaves
15 Black Peppercorns
4T White Wine
2T Olive Oil
1/2 Lemon, sliced
3 lbs. fresh Salmon Filets
1C Sour Cream
1/2C fresh Dill, chopped

Garnish:
Frisee
Cucumbers
Capers
Red Onions
Wheat or Pumpernickel Toast

Coat:
Breaking or bruising herbs releases extra flavor. Break the bay leaves in 2 or 3 pieces. Do not break them so small that they will be difficult to remove before serving. Mix the bay leaves, salt, brown sugar, dill, fennel, peppercorns, wine, oil, and lemon. Pack the mixture around the salmon, and wrap tightly in plastic wrap or aluminum foil.

Refrigerate 48 hours:
Let the salmon sit in a refrigerator overnight. Turn it over and let it sit overnight again. You are curing the salmon. After 48 hours, it will be perfectly fresh, and the seasonings will have spread throughout the fish.

When the salmon is cured, unwrap it, and rinse lightly. Remove the bay leaves and save the marinade for use in the fresh dill cream.

Mix:
Mix the reserved marinade, sour cream, and dill.

Serve:
Lay frisee in the center of a plate, and place the salmon on top. Arrange sliced cucumbers around the periphery, with capers and red onions around the edge. Set 3 pieces of wheat or pumpernickel toast, and 3 dabs of dill cream on the vegetables.

Serves 12

THE PHOENICIAN
THE TERRACE DINING ROOM
Scottsdale
Chef David Hough

SOFTSHELL CRAB AND CRABCAKE APPETIZER

1C Dungeness Crab Meat, any crab meat will do
2C fresh Cornbread Crumbs
1/2t Salt or Sonoran Seasoning
1/2t Ground Black Pepper
1t White Wine Worcestershire
1/2C Scallions, minced
1 Egg
1 Egg yolk
3T Chipotle Mayonnaise, recipe follows
3/4C Flour
2 Eggs, beaten
1C Cornbread Crumbs
3/4C Clarified Butter
4 Softshell Crabs, regular size

Garnish:
Southwestern Relish, recipe follows
Chipotle Mayonnaise, recipe follows

THE CRABCAKES

Form crabcakes:
Mix the Dungeness crab, 2C cornbread crumbs, salt, pepper, white wine Worcestershire, scallions, egg, yolk, and Chipotle Mayonnaise. Shape into 4 cakes.

Chill.

Coat:
Coat the chilled crabcakes with flour, 2 beaten eggs, and 1C cornbread crumbs. Reserve the remaining flour, egg, and crumbs for coating the crabs.

Fry several minutes:
Pan fry the crabcakes in butter over medium heat. Cook until nicely browned. When done, keep the liquids in the pan.

THE CRABS

Coat:
Coat the crabs with the reserved flour, egg, and cornbread.

Cook 3 to 4 minutes:
Saute the softshell crabs in the crabcake pan over medium heat or deep fry. Heat until light brown and fully cooked.

Serve:
Arrange a crab, crabcake, and Southwestern Relish on 4 plates, 7 inches each. Spoon a pool of Chipotle Mayonnaise on each plate. Use a piping sack to squeeze dots of red chile paste onto the mayonnaise. Draw a knife through the dots to make hearts.

Serves 4

CHIPOTLE MAYONNAISE

1C Mayonnaise
1/2t Sonoran Seasoning or Salt
2t Chipotle Paste
2T Wine Worcestershire
1t Red Chile Paste, or to taste

Combine and chill.

Yields 1C

(continued on next page)

SOUTHWESTERN RELISH

1 Red Bell Pepper, roasted and peeled
1 Zucchini
1 Yellow Squash
2 Scallions
1/2 bunch Cilantro
1 fresh Anaheim Chile
1/4C Black Olives
Juice from 1 Lime
1/4C Olive Oil
1T Sonoran Seasoning

Peel and dice:
Roast and peel the peppers. Several methods are described in the Appendix. Use the broil until skin turns black method. Dice all the vegetables.

Combine:
Toss with lime juice, olive oil, and seasoning.

SHERATON
TUCSON
EL CONQUISTADOR
Tucson
Chef Alan Zeman

BREADS

Cheddar Cheese and Onion Bread

French Bread

Fennel Toasts

Fry Bread

Southwestern Green Chile Corn Bread

Luxury Pumpkin Loaf

Zucchini Bread

Macy's Nondairy Peach Muffins

Vanilla Rolls

For more breads, please see index

CHEDDAR CHEESE AND ONION BREAD

A great substitute for garlic bread at your next barbecue!

2 loaves French Bread Dough, see recipe on page 27
1C Cheddar Cheese, shredded
1 bunch Green Onions, chopped
2 Eggs

Combine:
Using a knife, chop the cheese, onions, and eggs into the dough.
Form 2 loaves, leaving the dough loosely chopped. Place each loaf in
a 9-inch pie pan.

Let rise 1 hour:
Cover the loaves with a damp towel, and set in a warm place. Let
them rise until they double in size.

Bake 30 minutes:
Bake at 350 degrees.

Yields 2 loaves

**SWISS VILLAGE
BAKERY**
Payson
Chef Diana Mitchell

FRENCH BREAD

2T Shortening
2C Water
3C Bread Flour
3t Salt
1T Sugar
2 pkgs. Dry Yeast
1-3/4C to 2-3/4C Bread Flour
1/4C to 1/2C Bread Flour
1 Egg Yolk or Whole Egg
1T Water

Warm:
Heat the shortening with 2C water until just warmer than lukewarm.

Mix:
Mix 3C bread flour, salt, sugar, and yeast. Add the heated liquid to the flour mixture, and mix for 3 minutes, until a thin batter forms. Add just enough flour to make a stiff dough, about 1-3/4C to 2-3/4C.

Knead:
Sprinkle 1/4C to 1/2C flour, a little at a time, on a kneading surface. Knead for about 8 minutes, until the dough becomes smooth and elastic. For French bread, you will not need as much flour as you would use for white bread. Form 2 loaves. The loaves can be long and thin or standard bread shaped. French bread is typically made without bread pans.

Let rise 1 hour:
Cover the loaves with a damp towel, and set them in a warm place. Let the loaves rise until they double in size.

Bake 30 minutes:
Brush the loaves with a mixture of 1T water and 1 egg yolk or whole egg. Bake at 375 degrees.

Yields 2 loaves

SWISS VILLAGE BAKERY
Payson
Chef Diana Mitchell

FENNEL TOASTS

2 oz. whole Butter
3C fresh Fennel root, roughly chopped*
1/2C Onion, roughly chopped
1 clove Garlic, minced
Salt and Pepper, to taste
1 Baguette French bread, thinly sliced on the
  diagonal.

Garnish:
Baby Greens, such as Frisee, Arugula, and
  Mesquite

*Fennel root is most easily available around
  Thanksgiving and Christmas.

Saute several minutes:
Place the butter, fennel, onion, garlic, salt, and pepper in a sauce pan
over very low heat. Heat until the fennel and onions are completely
tender.

Puree.

Toast:
Toast the bread until it is crisp but not brown.

Serve:
Spread the fennel puree on crisp toasts. For a garnished presentation,
fold the toasts in half, and arrange them at the bottom of a plate,
from 4 to 8 o'clock. Fill the top of the plate with baby greens such as
frisee, arugula, and mesquite.

Serves 10

THE BOULDERS RESORT
LATILLA RESTAURANT
Carefree
Chef Brent E. Wertz

FRY BREAD

Fry bread is thicker and puffier than tortillas, but not as puffy as sopapillas.

10C Flour
4C Water
1/6C Baking Powder
1/4C Salt
Shortening, to coat pan

Knead:
Knead the flour, baking powder, salt, and water in a large bowl. Knead until soft, but not sticky.

Let sit 1/2 hour.

Form tortillas:
Portion the dough into balls the size of tennis balls. Sprinkle flour on wax paper, place one ball on the paper, and sprinkle flour on the ball. Use a rolling pin or the side of a bottle to form a 1/4 inch thick, plate-size tortilla. Repeat.

Fry 10 seconds each:
Heat 1 inch of shortening in a large frying pan to 180 degrees (very hot). Carefully place the tortillas in the hot oil. Cook to a golden brown on both sides, about 5 seconds each side.

Serve:
Fry bread is eaten with stews, soups, chili, roast beef sandwich filling, smothered in honey, or alone.

Serves 12 to 15

NAVAJO NATION INN
Window Rock
Chef Regis Tsosie

SOUTHWESTERN
GREEN CHILE CORN BREAD

1C Butter
3/4C Sugar
4 Eggs
1/2C Green Chilies, diced
1-1/2C Cream Style Corn
1/2C Cheddar Cheese, shredded
1/2C Jack Cheese, shredded
1C Flour
1C Yellow Cornmeal
2T Baking Powder
1t Salt

Mix:
In a mixer, cream the butter and sugar. Reduce the speed to slow. Add the eggs, one at a time. Add the chilies, corn, cheddar cheese, jack cheese, flour, cornmeal, baking powder and salt. Mix well.

Bake 1 hour:
Bake at 325 degrees in a well buttered 9-inch square pan.

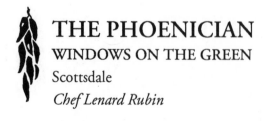

THE PHOENICIAN
WINDOWS ON THE GREEN
Scottsdale
Chef Lenard Rubin

LUXURY PUMPKIN LOAF

1/2 lb. Cream Cheese, softened
1/2C Butter, softened
2-1/2C Sugar
4 Eggs
2C Pumpkin, canned
3-1/2C Flour, all purpose
2t Baking Soda
1/2t Baking Powder
1t Salt
1t Cinnamon
1/2t Cloves
1C Pecans, chopped or pieces

Mix:
In a mixer, cream the cream cheese, butter, and sugar. Reduce the
speed to slow. Add the eggs one at a time, mixing well and scraping
the bowl after each egg. Add the pumpkin and mix.

In another bowl, combine the flour, baking soda, baking powder, salt,
cinnamon, cloves, and pecans. Stir until thoroughly mixed.

Pour the dry ingredients into the pumpkin batter all at once. Stir just
enough to thoroughly mix. Stirring too much will keep the bread
from being tender.

Bake 60 to 70 minutes:
Pour the batter into 2 greased bread pans. Bake at 350 degrees until
an inserted toothpick comes out clean.

Cool:
Cool the loaves in their pans for 10 minutes.
Remove and finish cooling on a rack.

Yields 2 loaves

JANOS
Tucson
Chef Janos Wilder

ZUCCHINI BREAD

2 Eggs
1C Sugar
1/2C Cottonseed or other Vegetable Oil
1C Zucchini, grated
1-1/2t Vanilla
1C Flour
1/2t Salt
1/2t Baking Soda, sifted
1/4t Baking Powder
1-1/2t Cinnamon
1/2C Walnuts, chopped

Mix:
Beat the eggs until light and foamy. Add the sugar, oil, zucchini, and vanilla. Mix for 1 minute. In another bowl, combine the flour, salt, baking soda, baking powder and cinnamon. Add the dry ingredients to the egg mixture and blend well. Stir in the walnuts.

Bake 70 minutes:
Pour the batter in a 2 lb. (standard) bread loaf pan, greased and dusted with flour. Bake at 300 degrees.

Yields 1 loaf

KEATON'S
RESTAURANT, GRILL AND BAR
Tucson

BUDDY'S GRILL
Tucson

BUSTER'S
RESTAURANT
Scottsdale and Flagstaff
Chef Tom Firth

MACY'S NONDAIRY PEACH MUFFINS

1C Whole Wheat Flour
1C Toasted Wheat Bran
1C Rolled Oats
1t ground Cinnamon
1t ground Nutmeg
1t ground Ginger
2-1/2t Baking Powder
3/4C Chopped Nuts or Seeds
   (Walnuts, Pecans, Sunflower Seeds)
3T Canola Oil
2/3C Honey
1/2C Apple Juice
1-1/2C fresh Peaches, diced*
1 Egg

*If you use frozen or canned peaches, be sure to
   drain them well.

Mix:

In a mixing bowl, combine the flour, bran, oats, cinnamon, nutmeg,
ginger, baking powder, and nuts. In another bowl, blend the oil,
honey, apple juice, peaches, and egg. Using a rubber spatula or
wooden spoon, fold the wet ingredients into the dry ingredients.
Be careful not to overmix. The batter should be wet and sticky, yet
hold its form when mounded into a muffin tin.

Bake 25 to 30 minutes:

Spoon the batter into a greased muffin tin so the batter is mounded
1/2 inch above the top of the tin. Bake at 325 degrees until golden
brown.

Serve:
Cool slightly before serving.

Yields 14 muffins

MACY'S
EUROPEAN COFFEE HOUSE
AND BAKERY
Flagstaff
Chef Sue-Bug Skelton

VANILLA ROLLS

1 pkg. Active Dry Yeast
3/4C Water
1/2C Sugar
2 Eggs, beaten
1/2C Crisco shortening
3C Flour
3T Vanilla
2T Butter, melted

Mix:
Dissolve the yeast in warm water. The water should not be much warmer than lukewarm (110 to 115 degrees), or the yeast will die. Stir in the sugar and eggs.

Place the shortening in a large bowl. Pour the yeast mixture on top and mix with a spoon. Gradually add the flour and vanilla, mixing in 1C flour and 1T vanilla at a time, until you have added 3C flour and 3T vanilla. Mix until a somewhat sticky dough is formed.

Form biscuits:
On a floured surface, roll the dough out to 1/4 inch thickness. Cut into biscuits with a biscuit cutter, and place the biscuits on a baking sheet. Pat each biscuit with a dab of melted butter and fold in half. Pinch closed.

Let rise 1 hour:
Set the biscuits in a warm place, cover them with a damp cloth, and let them rise until they double in bulk.

Bake 15 minutes:
Bake at 350 degrees.

Yields 3 Dozen

THE IMPECCABLE PIG
Scottsdale
Chef Shane Taggart

SALADS

Aldo Baldo Salad

Arugula and Tomato Salad

Mixed Green Salad with Parmesan
   Vinaigrette and Pine Nuts

Fresh Baby Lettuce Salad
   with Kiwi Vinaigrette

Cucumber Salad

Hareng Hollandaise

Southwestern Salad

Lobster Salad with
   Crisp Minted Cucumbers

Warm Calamari Salad

Campari Melon Salad

ALDO BALDO SALAD

Fresh fennel is most readily available during the Thanksgiving and Christmas seasons, making this a special holiday salad.

1/2 lb. Tuscan Salami
1/2 lb. Garbanzo Beans, cooked
3/4C Roma Tomatoes, julienne
1/2C Red Onion, slivered
2/3C fresh Fennel root, slivered
1/4C fresh Basil, slivered
1C Italian Vinaigrette
1/8C Balsamic Vinegar
Salt and Pepper, to taste

Mix well.

Serves 8 to 10

ALDO BALDO
Scottsdale
Chef Joseph DeLucia

ARUGULA AND TOMATO SALAD

2C Arugula*
1/2C Red Onion
8 Roma Tomatoes, julienne
1T Garlic, minced
1C Olive Oil
3T Balsamic Vinegar
1/2t Salt
1/4t Pepper, freshly ground

* Arugula is a leafy green herb. Romaine lettuce
makes a nice substitute in this recipe.

Mix well.

Serves 4

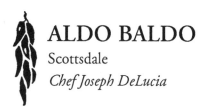

ALDO BALDO
Scottsdale
Chef Joseph DeLucia

MIXED GREEN SALAD WITH PARMESAN VINAIGRETTE AND PINE NUTS

Mixed Greens, enough for two servings
  (Frisee, Red and Green Oak, Mache, Boston
  Bibb, etc.)
2T Pine Nuts
6T Parmesan Vinaigrette Dressing, recipe follows
Fresh ground Pepper, to taste
1T Parmesan Cheese

Toss the greens, nuts, dressing, and pepper. Sprinkle cheese on top.

PARMESAN VINAIGRETTE DRESSING

4T Red Wine Vinegar
1T Mustard
1 small Shallot, diced
Juice of 1/2 Lemon
2 leaves fresh Basil, cut in small pieces
2T Parmesan Cheese
1-1/8C Olive Oil

Mix all the ingredients, adding the oil last. Whisk in the oil in a
slow, steady stream.

Serves 2

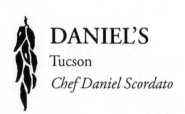

DANIEL'S
Tucson
Chef Daniel Scordato

FRESH BABY LETTUCE SALAD WITH KIWI VINAIGRETTE

1 head Baby Lolla Rosa
1 head Green Oak
1 head Red Oak
1/4 head Frisee
Fresh Herbs
Croutons
Tomato Wedges

Arrange:
Wash the greens in ice water and carefully shake dry. Cut off the bottom end of each head and arrange on a salad plate. Garnish with fresh herbs, croutons, and tomato wedges.
Serves 4

KIWI VINAIGRETTE

2 Kiwis, coarsely chopped
1/2C Red Wine Vinegar
1/4C Midori*
1 Egg Yolk
1 clove Garlic, minced
1T Lemon Juice
1t Salt
1/4C Chives, diced
3/4C Olive Oil

Garnish:
Kiwi slices

* Midori is a melon liqueur.

Mix:
Mix all the ingredients except the olive oil. Whisk the olive oil into the mixture slowly. Pour the dressing over salad and garnish with whole kiwi slices.

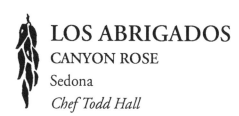

LOS ABRIGADOS
CANYON ROSE
Sedona
Chef Todd Hall

CUCUMBER SALAD

2C Cucumbers, marked by carving fork lines down
   sides, then sliced
2 large Red Onions, cut into rings
1 stalk Celery, diced
2 Green Peppers, diced
3/4C Sugar
1/3C Water
Salt, to taste
1/3C Salad Oil
1/2C White Vinegar

Heat:
In a saucepan over low flame, heat all the ingredients except the oil
and vinegar until the sugar dissolves. Stir as you heat.

Let sit 2 hours:
Mix in the oil and vinegar. Let sit at room temperature.

Chill.

Serves 12

NAUTICAL INN
Lake Havasu City
Chef Elaine Perritt

HARENG HOLLANDAISE
Dutch Herring Salad

22 oz. pickled Herring filets, diced small
2 large tart Green Apples, diced
1 medium Red Onion, diced
1T Lemon Juice
1T Sugar
2C Sour Cream
1t White Pepper
1t Parsley Flakes

Garnish:
Lettuce
Tomato
Hard Boiled Egg
Olive
Pickles

Mix well. Serve on a bed of garnished lettuce.

Serves 6 to 8

COTTAGE PLACE
Flagstaff
Chef Kurt Gottschalk

SOUTHWESTERN SALAD

2 Chayote, peeled*
1/4 lb. Chorizo
2T Lime Juice
6T Olive Oil
1t Jalapeño, minced
1 clove Garlic, crushed
Salt and Pepper, to taste
Raddicchio, Spinach or other interesting
   combination of greens
Croutons, recipe follows

* Chayote is a southwestern squash. If not available,
  substitute zucchini, cooked al dente.

Fry:
Fry the chorizo. Save 2T drippings for the next step.

Heat:
In a saute pan, heat the chorizo drippings, lime juice, olive oil,
jalapeño, garlic, salt, and pepper. Heat until just hot.

Blanch:
Blanch the chayote for about 1 minute in boiling water. Slice.

Serve:
Arrange the greens on a salad plate. Top with chayote, chorizo, and
warm dressing. Serve croutons on the side.

Serves 8

CROUTONS

1 baguette French Bread, sliced 1/8" to 1/4"
Butter, to taste
4 oz. Goat Cheese
1T Cilantro, minced
1 clove Garlic, crushed
1t Ancho Chili Powder
Salt and Pepper, to taste

Toast:
Brush the bread slices with butter and toast in oven.

Top:
Mix the cheese, cilantro, garlic, chili powder, salt, and pepper.
Spread the mixture on the toasted croutons.

Serves 8

CAFE
TERRA COTTA
Tucson
Chef Donna Nordin

LOBSTER SALAD WITH CRISP MINTED CUCUMBERS

Crisp Marinated Cucumbers with Mint, recipe
 follows
2 Lobsters, 1-1/2 lbs. each
5 Plum Tomatoes, cut into 6 slices each
Freshly ground Black Pepper
1 bunch Watercress

Prepare cucumbers:
Recipe below.

Boil 7 to 8 minutes:
Boil the lobsters. When fully cooked, remove the meat from the
shells, and set the meat aside.

Season:
Dip the tomato slices in the reserved cucumber marinade. Sprinkle
the tomatoes with pepper.

Assemble salad:
Set out six 10-inch plates. Place 5 tomato slices on each plate,
arranging them as hour numerals on a clock. Between each tomato,
lay 5 little piles of minted cucumber.

Dip the watercress in marinade. Lay 2 sprigs on each tomato,
pointing the stems towards the center of the plate. Dip the lobster in
marinade and lay some in the center of each plate.

Chill.

Serve:
Dress with marinade, if desired.

Yields 6 small Salads or Appetizers

CRISP MARINATED CUCUMBERS WITH MINT

2 large hothouse Cucumbers, peeled and sliced thin
1-1/2t Kosher Salt
1/2C Rice Vinegar
3T Safflower Oil
1 clove Garlic, minced
1/8t freshly ground White Pepper
3-4T Fresh Mint, chopped

Marinate 1 hour:
Sprinkle the cucumbers with salt. Set aside in a perforated pan or colander for 1 hour.

Chill:
Squeeze the cucumbers dry. Mix the vinegar, oil, garlic, and white pepper. Add the cucumbers and toss. Chill well.

Serve:
When chilled, drain the cucumbers. Save the marinade. Some will be used in assembling the salad, above, and the remainder may be used to dress the salad. Add mint to the cucumbers. The cucumbers can also be served on their own as a summer salad.

THE BOULDERS
RESORT
LATILLA RESTAURANT
Carefree
Chef Brent E. Wertz

WARM CALAMARI SALAD

1 lb. Calamari
1 Tomato, peeled, seeded, and chopped
2 Shallots, minced
1/2t Garlic, minced
2 Green Onions, sliced fine
1T Cilantro, chopped
2T Dijon Mustard, extra strong
1/2C Red Wine Vinegar
2C Olive Oil
Salt, to taste
Pinch of Black Pepper

Garnish:
Mixed Greens
Lime or Tomato Wedges
Warm Corn Chips

Prepare the calamari:
Remove and discard the calamari eyes and beak. For easier
handling, do not separate the tentacles. Rinse to remove any sand.
Slice the body into thin rings. Do not slice the tentacles.

Mix the dressing:
Whisk the mustard and vinegar together in a bowl. Slowly whisk in
the olive oil. Reserve a little dressing for the garnish.

Bring to boil:
Add salt to a pot of water until it tastes almost as salty as the ocean
(quite salty). Bring the water to a boil. Drop the calamari into the
boiling water and stir. When the water starts to simmer again
(about 1 minute), drain.

Toss:

In another bowl, toss the hot calamari, dressing, tomato, shallots, garlic, onions, and cilantro. Season with salt and pepper. The calamari may already be salty enough after boiling, so you may not need to use any salt.

Serve:

On a serving plate, arrange the calamari next to mixed greens. Lightly dress the greens with the reserved dressing. Garnish with lime or tomato wedges and serve immediately with warm corn chips.

Yields 4 Appetizers or 6 Salads with greens

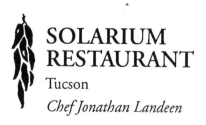

SOLARIUM
RESTAURANT
Tucson
Chef Jonathan Landeen

CAMPARI MELON SALAD

1 Honeydew Melon, 1/2 inch diced
1 Cantalope Melon, 1/2 inch diced
1T Campari*
3T fresh Basil, julienne

*Campari is an Italian liqueur.

Mix well.

Serves 4 to 6

ALDO BALDO
Scottsdale
Chef Joseph DeLucia

SAUCES, DRESSINGS & CONDIMENTS

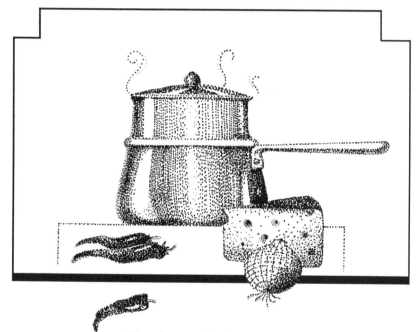

Chardonnay Leek Sauce
Tomato Vodka Cream Sauce
Hazelnut Sauce
Italian Vinaigrette
Cucumber Dill Relish
Cantaloupe Chutney
Quick Remoulade
For more recipes, please see index

CHARDONNAY LEEK SAUCE

Chardonnay Leek Sauce is wonderful on poultry.

    1 medium leek, chopped, save the top
    6T Shallots
    1C Chardonnay
    2T Butter

    Garnish:
    Strips of leek top

Saute 3 minutes:
Saute the leek, shallots, and Chardonnay over medium heat. Cook until the leek becomes translucent. Strain. Add the butter.

Serve:
Garnish with strips of leek top.

LOEWS VENTANA CANYON RESORT
VENTANA ROOM
Tucson
Chef Takashi Shiramizu

TOMATO VODKA CREAM SAUCE

This sauce is delicious on Linguine with Smoked Salmon (see Seafood) or Spinach Ravioli.

> 1T Olive Oil, heated
> 1/2C Shallots
> 1C Vodka
> 2 qts. Heavy Cream
> 3 Tomatoes, chopped
> 1/4C Lobster Base*
> Salt and Pepper, to taste

> *Lobster base can be purchased in gourmet stores, or you can use fish stock (see Seafood).

Saute and simmer 20 to 30 minutes:
Saute the shallots in oil over a medium flame until translucent. Add the vodka and reduce by 1/2. Add the cream and tomatoes. Reduce by 2/3. Do not let the cream boil over the sides of the saucepan. Add lobster base, salt, and pepper.

Serves 10 to 15

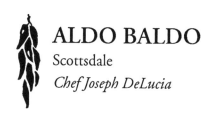

ALDO BALDO
Scottsdale
Chef Joseph DeLucia

HAZELNUT SAUCE

An attractive, mellow poultry topping, hazelnut sauce is also wonderful on vanilla ice cream.

> 3/4C Frangelico
> 4T Molasses
> 3C Heavy Cream
> 1/2C Hazelnuts*
> Salt and Pepper, to taste
> Dash of Cinnamon and Nutmeg, if desired

> *You can buy roasted, peeled hazelnuts in
> some markets.

Roast, peel, and chop:
Roast the nuts in a 325 degree oven for about 6 minutes until browned. Peel and chop.

Simmer 25 minutes:
In a saucepan, slowly simmer the Frangelico and molasses for a few minutes until the sauce is reduced by half. Add the cream and reduce by half again, about 20 minutes. When done, the sauce should have a medium consistency. Add the nuts, salt, pepper, and if desired, add cinnamon and nutmeg.

Yields 2 Cups

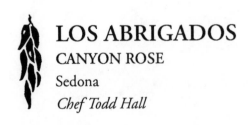 **LOS ABRIGADOS**
CANYON ROSE
Sedona
Chef Todd Hall

ITALIAN VINAIGRETTE

2C Olive Oil
1/2C Red Wine Vinegar
1/8C Oregano, chopped
1/4C Basil, chopped
1-1/2t Thyme, chopped
1T Garlic
1-1/2t Salt
1-1/2t Pepper

Mix well and adjust seasonings to taste.

To make a cheesy vinaigrette:
Add 1C Parmesan cheese directly to the dressing, or sprinkle cheese on top of the dressing when serving the salad.

Yields 3 Cups

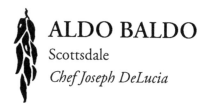

ALDO BALDO
Scottsdale
Chef Joseph DeLucia

CUCUMBER DILL RELISH
FOR FRESH SEAFOOD

Cucumber Dill Relish is a heart healthy accompaniment for seafood. It is one of our guests' most popular requests.

> **1 Cucumber, peeled, seeded and chopped fine**
> **1-1/2T Fresh Dillweed, chopped**
> **1C Yogurt, plain**
> **1t Honey**
> **1t Dijon Mustard**
> **Salt, to taste**

Combine and blend well.

Yields 1-1/2 cups

KEATON'S
RESTAURANT, GRILL AND BAR
Tucson

BUDDY'S GRILL
Tucson

BUSTER'S
RESTAURANT
Scottsdale and Flagstaff

Chef Tom Firth

CANTALOUPE CHUTNEY

Cantaloupe Chutney is a delicious condiment with chicken or fresh fish. Use your imagination to serve chutney with other favorite dishes.

1 medium Cantaloupe, diced
1 medium Pineapple, decored and diced
1/4C Brown Sugar
1/4C Red Wine Vinegar
1/4C Sherry
1/4C Marsala
1/4C Brandy
1T Curry
1T Cloves, ground
1T Ginger, crushed

Simmer 1 hour:
Bring to a slow boil, and cook over medium heat, stirring occasionally, until the chutney develops the consistency of jam.

Chill.

Serves 8

THE
IMPECCABLE PIG
Scottsdale
Chef Shane Taggart

QUICK REMOULADE

Quick Remoulade goes well with seafood, especially chilled shrimp or crab claws.

> 1C Ground Mustard, with whole seeds, Creole is
>   best
> 1/2C Dijon Mustard, extra strong
> 1/2C Ketchup
> 1/3C Red Wine Vinegar
> Juice from 2 Lemons
> 1T Horseradish
> 3T Parsley, chopped
> Tabasco Sauce, to taste

Blend well.

Yields 2-1/2C

SOLARIUM RESTAURANT
Tucson
Chef Jonathan Landeen

SIDE DISHES

Squash Williamsburg

Honey Mustard Greens

Sauteed Spinach with Garlic and Parmesan Cheese

Scalloped Potatoes

Bohn Jon Bouranee

Shallots

Blue Cheese Coleslaw

Vegetable Garnish

For more side dishes, please see index

SQUASH WILLIAMSBURG
(OR SEDONA)

A great holiday vegetable side dish!

  1 Butternut Squash, cut into 2 inch chunks
  1 Yellow Onion, halved, sliced, and sauteed
   until clear
  1C fresh Pineapple, diced
  1t Lemon Juice
  1T Brown Sugar
  1 Egg
  1 pinch Nutmeg
  1 pinch Cinnamon
  1 pinch Allspice
  1 pinch Cloves
  1/4C Pecans, chopped
  1/4C Red Bell Pepper, diced

Mix:
Mix all the ingredients except the pecans and bell pepper.

Bake 20 to 30 minutes:
Place the mixture in a shallow baking pan. Sprinkle with pecans and red bell pepper. Bake at 375 degrees until firm.

Serves 6 to 8

 **OAK CREEK OWL**
Sedona
Chef Sean Cooke

HONEY
MUSTARD GREENS

1 lb. Mustard Greens
1 oz. whole Butter
1/4C Shallots, chopped
3T Honey
Salt and Pepper, to taste

Heat several minutes:
Blanch the mustard greens slightly. Drain. Place the greens, butter, and shallots in a saute pan. Cook over low heat 2 to 3 minutes. Add the honey, salt, and pepper.

Serves 5

**THE BOULDERS
RESORT**
LATILLA RESTAURANT
Carefree
Chef Brent E. Wertz

SAUTEED SPINACH WITH GARLIC AND PARMESAN CHEESE

1T Butter
1 clove Garlic, finely chopped
2 heads fresh Spinach leaves
1T Parmesan Cheese
1/2T Parmesan Cheese

Saute several minutes:
Heat the garlic and butter in a large sauce pan, for a few seconds. Swirl the pan over medium high heat until the garlic is hot, but not brown. Add the spinach. Stack the leaves high in the pan; they will wilt during cooking. Toss and heat the spinach until all the leaves are wilted.

Remove from heat and drain excess water from pan. Mix in 1T Parmesan cheese.

Serve:
Place the spinach in bowls and sprinkle with 1/2T Parmesan cheese.

Serves 2

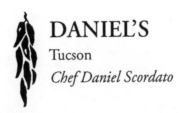

DANIEL'S
Tucson
Chef Daniel Scordato

SCALLOPED POTATOES

4 large Potatoes, peeled and sliced
2T Flour, all purpose
2T Parsley, chopped
Flour
Parsley
Nutmeg
Salt
Pepper
1C whole Milk
2T Butter
1C Vermont White Cheddar Cheese

Assemble layers:
Place 1 layer of potatoes on the bottom of a greased 10-inch baking pan. Sprinkle the potatoes with flour, parsley, nutmeg, salt, and pepper. Continue to layer until the pan is 3/4 full.

Heat:
Heat the milk and butter over low heat until hot.

Bake 1-3/4 to 2 hours:
Pour the milk mixture over the potatoes. Sprinkle cheddar on top. Bake at 350 degrees until golden brown.

Serves 6

THE BOULDERS RESORT
LATILLA RESTAURANT
Carefree
Chef Brent E. Wertz

BOHN JON BOURANEE
Eggplant

This dish is a traditional Afghani compliment to Kabali Palaw (see Poultry).

Bohn Jon Bouranee can also be prepared with yellow squash or pumpkin instead of eggplant. Follow the same directions, but add 1t sugar and 1t tumeric to the red sauce.

> 1 Eggplant, cut in 1/2 inch slices
> 1t Oil
> 1 Onion
> 1/2t Oil
> 2T Tomato, crushed
> 1t Salt
> 1t Coriander
> 1t Garlic
> 1t Black Pepper
> 1/2C Sour Cream
> 1/2C Plain Yogurt
> 1/2t Salt
> 1/2t Garlic, fresh minced

Saute:
Saute the eggplant in 1t oil. Use low heat if the slices are thick, or high heat for thin slices. Saute until the eggplant is brown but not mushy. When done, remove the eggplant, and blot the oil in a paper towel.

Puree:
Puree 1 onion with 1/2t oil.

Heat 15 minutes:
Saute the pureed onion until golden. Add the tomato, salt, coriander, garlic, and pepper. Add enough water to make sauce the consistency of a thin puree. Simmer for a moment. Pour the sauce on the eggplant. Cover, and simmer slowly for 10 minutes. The eggplant will begin to absorb the sauce.

Mix the white sauce:
In a bowl, mix the sour cream, yogurt, salt, and garlic.

Serve:
Spread 2/3 of the white sauce on a platter. Place the eggplant on top. Artfully add the remaining white sauce.

Serves 2 to 4

CHOPANDAZ
AFGHANI
CUISINE
Tempe
Chef Shuja Ahmad

SHALLOTS

10 Shallots, cut into rings
1C Flour
1t Cayenne Pepper
1t Salt
1t Black Pepper

Coat:
Coat the shallot rings in a mixture of flour, cayenne pepper, salt, and black pepper.

Deep Fry:
Deep fry until golden brown.

Serves 3 to 6

**THE BOULDERS
RESORT**
LATILLA RESTAURANT
Carefree
Chef Brent E. Wertz

BLUE CHEESE
COLE SLAW

5-6C Green Cabbage, grated
1/2C Carrots, grated
2C Dry Curd Cottage Cheese
1C Toasted Round Croutons
Blue Cheese Dressing

Toss.

Serves 6 to 8

**RANCHO DE LOS
CABALLEROS**
Wickenburg
Chef Daniel Martin

VEGETABLE GARNISH

Vegetable Garnish and Fried Leek are a full complement to Braised Salmon (Seafood) or other light entrees.

> **6 oz. Purple Peruvian Potatoes (2 medium)***
> **1/3C Salt**
> **4T Butter**
> **3 small Carrots, peeled**
> **3 small Parsnips, peeled**
> **6 sprigs Thyme or 1/4t minced**
> **Pinch of Sugar**
> **4T Chicken Stock**
> **Salt and cracked White Pepper, lightly to taste**
> **1/2C Fava Beans**
> **1/2C Chicken Stock**
> **3 oz. Butter**
> **Salt and cracked White Pepper**

> *Substitute baby Red Boiling Potatoes if Purple
>   Peruvian are not available.

Boil:
Rinse the potatoes and place them in 1 gallon of cold water with 1/3C salt. Bring to a boil, then reduce heat and simmer until cooked. Cool the cooked potatoes in cold running water. Cut into 1/4 inch angled slices. Set aside.

Saute and simmer 6 to 10 minutes:
Heat 2T butter in each of 2 pans. Place the carrots in one pan, and the parsnips in the other. Add 3 sprigs of thyme to each, and lightly season with salt, pepper, and a pinch of sugar. When the vegetables sizzle, deglaze with 4T chicken stock. Simmer until the vegetables are soft, but not mushy, and the liquid becomes a nearly dry glaze. Set aside.

Remove skins:
Remove the beans from their shells. Blanch for 15 seconds in boiling, salted water, then shock in ice water. Remove the skins. Save the beans in a covered container.

Simmer 12 to 18 minutes:
Place the potato, carrots, and parsnips, and 1/2C chicken stock in a saucepan. Bring to a boil, reduce heat and simmer until the potatoes are hot, and the sauce turns to glaze. Add the beans, salt, and white pepper, and cook until the beans are warm.

Serves 4

FRIED LEEK

Fried leek can be served as a garnish for the vegetables above, or they can be served on their own as an appetizer.

> 1 medium Leek
> 2T Flour
> Salt, to taste

Coat and deep fry:
Remove the green outer layer of the leek. Cut it in half lengthwise, then cut 3-inch julienne strips. Rinse well in cold water, and pat dry. Coat the strips in flour. Remove any excess flour, and deep fry. When golden brown, place them on a paper towel, and season with salt. To keep the leek crisp, set in a warm place until ready to serve.

Serves 4

THE PHOENICIAN
MARY ELAINE'S
Scottsdale
Chef Alessandro Stratta

MICHAEL'S SALSA WITH TORTILLA CHIPS

13 oz. can Stewed Tomatoes
1/4C Onion, diced
2T Red Wine Vinegar
1/4C Hot Green Chili, diced
1-1/2t Garlic Salt
1-1/2t Onion Salt
1-1/2t Cumin, ground
1/4C Jalapeño Peppers with juice
1/8t Red Chili
Tortilla Chips, recipe below

Combine all the ingredients and refrigerate overnight.
Serve with tortilla chips.

Yields 1 Quart

TORTILLA CHIPS

1 pkg. Corn Tortillas, 6-inch diameter
Chili Powder, to taste
Garlic Salt, to taste

Deep fry:
Cut the tortillas into eighths. Fry in hot oil for a moment until
golden. Blot the oil with paper towels.
Sprinkle with chili powder and
garlic salt.

MICHAEL'S FINE DINING
Page
Chef Michael J. Decker

SOUPS

Roasted Corn Bisque
Ham Florentine Soup
Red Rock Chowder
Smoked Salmon Green Onion Cream Bisque
Black and White Bean Soup
Roasted Sweet Pepper Bisque with Papaya
  Red Onion Relish & Lemon Aioli
Chicken, Lime and Tortilla Soup
Chilled Gazpacho Soup
Green Chile Soup
Cream of Jalapeno Soup
Creamy Sweet Potato Jalapeño Soup
Cream of Mushroom Soup
Swiss Onion Soup
Leek Bisque Soup
Brandied Onion Bisque

ROASTED CORN BISQUE

5C Niblet Corn (1 lb.)
5C Sweet Cream Corn
2C Water
5 Anaheim Green Chilies, chopped
5 Jalapeños, minced
1t Shallots, minced
1C canned Green Chilies, chopped
1/2C Bacon
1t Cilantro, chopped
1 pinch Oregano, fresh
1 pinch Basil, fresh
1 oz. Tabasco
2 pinches Albuquerque Chili Pepper or Cayenne
2 pinches dark red Chili Pepper Powder
1t Sugar
1t Worcestershire Sauce
1T Chicken Bouillon Granules
2t Cumin
Salt and Pepper, to taste
Cream, if needed
Garnish:
Chopped Chives
Cream

Roast 20 minutes:
Spread the corn on a sheet pan and bake at 350 degrees. (You may toss the corn in olive oil before baking.) To test for doneness, bite a piece. It is done when it feels slightly hard and sticks to your teeth.

Saute 15 minutes:
Saute corn with remaining ingredients (except cream) over high heat.

Puree:
Puree the mixture until silky smooth. Thin with cream, if necessary.

Reheat and serve:
Garnish with chopped chives and a little cream.

Serves 10

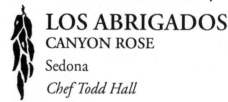

LOS ABRIGADOS
CANYON ROSE
Sedona
Chef Todd Hall

HAM FLORENTINE SOUP

A great holiday soup!

3T Flour
3T Butter
1 medium Yellow Onion, diced
3C Chicken Broth
1C Pineapple Juice
1t Salt
1/2t White Pepper
1/2t fresh Garlic, minced
3 drops Worcestershire
3 drops Tabasco
1/2C Ham, 1/4 inch cubes
1C fresh Spinach, chopped
1/4C Heavy Cream

Garnish:
Pineapple, diced
Red Bell Pepper, diced

Heat 15 to 20 minutes:
Cook the flour and butter over low heat until a nutty aroma
develops. Remove the roux from heat. In another pan, saute the
onion until it becomes translucent. Add the broth, pineapple juice,
salt, white pepper, garlic, Worcestershire, Tabasco, and ham. Bring
to a simmer. Stir in the roux and simmer 5 minutes.

Stir in:
Remove from heat, and stir in the spinach and cream.

Serve:
Garnish with pineapple
and red bell pepper.

OAK CREEK OWL
Sedona
Chef Sean Cooke

Serves 6 to 8

RED ROCK CHOWDER

This is Mr. Cooke's version of a Creole-style soup.

Your favorite Rice, to yield 1/2C
1/2C Whitefish, 1/2 inch cubes
Butter or Oil, to coat pan
2T Butter
2T Flour
1 small Red Onion, diced
1 stick Celery, diced
1 fresh Anaheim Chile, diced
1 Yellow Bell Pepper, diced
1t Oregano, whole
1t Rosemary, ground
1t fresh Garlic, minced
1/2t Tarragon, whole
1/2t Cayenne, or to taste
1/4t White Pepper
1/2t Salt
1/4C Tomatoes, diced
1/2C Tomato Sauce
3 drops Worcestershire
3 drops Tabasco
1C Chicken Broth
1C Clam Juice
1/2C Clams

Preparation:
Steam the rice.

Saute the whitefish in butter or oil. When done, drain the butter, and rinse the fish with cold water.

Prepare the roux by heating 2T butter until very hot. Stir in 2T flour, and cook over a low flame, stirring frequently until the roux turns red-brown. If black specks develop, start over. Refrigerate until ready to use.

Heat 10 to 15 minutes:
In a large saucepan, saute the onion, celery, chile, and yellow pepper. Add the remaining ingredients, except the clams. Bring to a simmer. Add the roux, stirring constantly, and simmer 5 minutes. Add the rice, whitefish, and clams. Heat until hot.

Serve:
Serve hot.

Serves 6 to 8

OAK CREEK OWL
Sedona
Chef Sean Cooke

SMOKED SALMON GREEN ONION CREAM BISQUE

3T Brown Sugar
2T Chili Powder
2t Salt
1t Garlic Powder
6 oz. Salmon*
4T ripe Tomatoes, diced
4 oz. wild Mushrooms (a few)
1/4t Garlic
1T Olive Oil
4 pieces Puff Pastry
1 Egg Yolk, beaten
Green Onion Cream, recipe follows

*You can buy salmon that is already cured and
smoked, but it may not be as wonderful.

Let sit 1 hour:
Mix the brown sugar, chili powder, salt and garlic powder in a bowl.
Rub the mixture into the salmon flesh. Let sit at room temperature 1
hour.

Smoke 1 hour:
Smoke the salmon over smoldering, but not hot, mesquite. Cook
until medium rare.

Prepare Green Onion Cream.

Saute few minutes:
Lightly grill or saute the mushrooms and garlic in olive oil.

Bake 25 minutes:
Place the salmon, cream, and mushrooms in 4 oven safe bowls.
Cover with puff pastry, sealing the pastry edges over the bowl rims.
Brush the pastry with egg yolk. Bake at 400 degrees until the pastries
form domes and turn golden brown.

Serves 4

GREEN ONION CREAM

1 large Yellow Onion with white ends, root tip
  removed
1 bunch Scallions
1t Garlic, freshly minced
Butter, to coat pan
8T Sherry
2C Chicken Stock
1C fresh Spinach
Sherry, to taste
Salt and Pepper, to taste

Heat:
Saute the onions, scallions, and garlic in butter until the onions
are translucent. Add the sherry and chicken stock. Swish for a
moment, then cook until the volume is reduced by 2/3.

Puree:
Strain the heated mixture. Keep the sauce in the pan. Puree the
solids with spinach.

Add and cool:
Mix the puree into the sauce. Add salt, pepper, and sherry to taste.
Cool.

JANOS
Tucson
Chef Janos Wilder

BLACK AND WHITE BEAN SOUP

The black and white beans are kept separate until serving, when they are combined for a unique presentation.

1C small White Beans
1C Black Beans
1 Ham Hock
4 Smoked Pork Loin Steaks
1T fresh Thyme
1 Bay Leaf
2 cloves Garlic, finely diced

Broth:
4T Olive Oil
4 oz. Panchetta (Italian Bacon) or regular smoked
  bacon, diced
1/2C Carrots, diced
1/2C Onions, diced
1/2C Celery, diced
1/2C Red Pepper, diced
1/2C Green Pepper, diced
2 qts. Chicken Stock

2T Vinegar
1 bunch Parsley, chopped
Pepper, to taste
Salt, to taste

Soak overnight:
Place the black beans in one pot and the white beans in another. Add warm water and soak overnight. When done, drain, and return the beans to their pots.

Simmer 2-1/2 hours:
In a bowl, mix the ham hock, pork loin, thyme, bay leaf, and garlic.

Place half the mixture in each bean pot. Simmer 2-1/2 hours, until the beans are soft. When done, remove the meat, and set it aside. Leave the beans in the pots.

Heat bacon-vegetable broth:
In one pan, saute the Panchetta in olive oil until golden brown. Add the carrots, onions, celery, red pepper and green pepper. Cook until the vegetables are glazed. Add the chicken stock and cook on high for 5 minutes.

Heat 20 to 30 minutes:
Add half of the bacon-vegetable broth and 1T vinegar to each bean pot. Simmer 15 to 25 minutes. Bone the cooked meat and cut into small cubes. Add half the meat, half the parsley, and pepper to each pot. Bring to a boil. Season with salt.

Serve:
Using 2 ladles, pour the soups at the same time, side by side, into one bowl. The black bean soup will stay on one side of the bowl, and the white bean soup will fill the other.

Serves 8

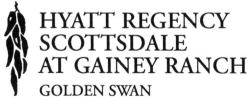

HYATT REGENCY
SCOTTSDALE
AT GAINEY RANCH
GOLDEN SWAN
Scottsdale
Chef Anton Brunbauer

ROASTED SWEET PEPPER BISQUE WITH PAPAYA RED ONION RELISH AND LEMON AIOLI

4 Red Bell Peppers, roasted, peeled,
    seeded, and diced
4 Green Bell Peppers, diced
4 Yellow Sweet Peppers, diced
4T Safflower Oil
3/4C Onions, diced
1/2C Carrots, diced
1/2C Celery, diced
3T fresh Oregano, chopped
3T fresh Chives, chopped
3T fresh Basil, chopped
3T fresh Marjoram, chopped
2 Cloves Garlic
3 qts. Chicken Stock
2T Lemon Juice
2T Malted Vinegar
2t Salt
1t Pepper

Garnish:
Papaya and Red Onion Relish, recipe follows
Lemon Aioli, recipe follows

Simmer 20 minutes:
Cook all but the last four ingredients over medium heat in a large pot.
Simmer until the liquid is reduced by 1/3.

Puree:
Puree the sauteed vegetables. Mix in the lemon juice, vinegar, salt and pepper. Adjust the seasonings to taste.

Serve:
Spoon 1T Papaya and Red Onion Relish on each 8 ounce bowl of bisque. Drizzle Lemon Aioli on top.

Serves 12

PAPAYA AND RED ONION RELISH

1 Papaya, diced small
1/4 Jicama, diced small
1/2 small Red Onion, diced small
1/2 bunch Cilantro, chopped
1 Green Onion, diced small
Juice of 1 Lime
Salt and Pepper, to taste

Combine.

LEMON AIOLI

1 Egg Yolk
1/2t Garlic, minced
1t Dijon Mustard
1/2C Extra Virgin Olive Oil
Juice of 1/2 Lemon
Salt and Pepper, to taste

Mix:
Beat the egg yolk, garlic, and mustard together in a mixer. Reduce the speed to low. Slowly add the oil, then lemon juice, then salt, and pepper. If the aioli is too thick, add hot water.

THE BOULDERS
RESORT
LATILLA RESTAURANT
Carefree
Chef Brent E. Wertz

CHICKEN, LIME AND TORTILLA SOUP

3C Chicken Stock or Broth
Juice of 2 Limes
1/2C Tomato Juice
1 Jalapeño, chopped
1 bunch Cilantro, chopped
1 Green Onion, chopped
1/4 lb. boneless, skinless Chicken Breast,
  cut in strips
1C Corn Oil, hot
1/2C Hominy
Salt and ground Black Pepper, to taste

Garnish:
2 Corn Tortillas, small julienne
1 Avocado, diced
1C Jack Cheese, shredded

Simmer, grill, and deep fry, 1 hour total:
Simmer the stock, lime juice, tomato juice, jalapeño, cilantro, and
green onion 1 hour. Meanwhile, grill the chicken strips until done.
Dice the cooked strips into 1-inch cubes and set aside. Deep fry the
tortilla strips in corn oil until crisp. Set aside. When the broth is
done, add the chicken, hominy, salt, and pepper. Heat until hot.

Serve:
Garnish with the tortilla strips, avocado, and cheese.

Serves 4

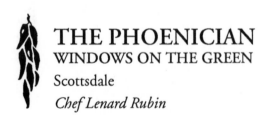

THE PHOENICIAN
WINDOWS ON THE GREEN
Scuttsdale
Chef Lenard Rubin

80

CHILLED
GAZPACHO SOUP

1-3/4 lb. fresh Tomatoes, coarsely chopped
  or 2 cans sliced Baby Tomatoes, 14.5 oz. each
15 oz. can pitted Black Olives, 3 slices each
2 cloves fresh Garlic, minced
3T Red Wine Vinegar
1t Worcestershire Sauce
1-1/2T Maggi Seasoning*
1-1/2C Beef Stock or 10.5 oz. can Beef Broth
3/4C Chablis Wine
Tabasco Sauce, to taste

Garnish:
Croutons
Chives, chopped

*Maggi seasoning can be purchased in Oriental
 markets.

Chill 24 hours:
Combine all the ingredients. Chill 24 hours. Garnish with croutons
and chopped chives.

Serves 6

THE TACK ROOM
Tucson
The Kane and Vactor Family

GREEN CHILE SOUP

A heart-healthy soup.

> 1 clove Garlic, diced
> 1 large White Onion, diced
> 3 medium Potatoes, diced into 1/2 inch pieces,
>   skins on
> 2 medium Tomatoes, diced into 1/2 inch pieces
> 3 qts. Water or clarified Chicken Stock
> 8 fresh Anaheim Chilies, roasted and peeled,
>   or 8 canned Chilies
> 4 Green Onions
> 4 to 5T Cilantro, chopped
> Salt and Pepper, to taste

Saute several minutes:
Saute the garlic, white onion, potatoes and tomatoes in vegetable oil until the onions are transparent.

Heat 20 minutes:
Place the sauteed vegetables and water or chicken stock in a large kettle. Bring to a low boil, cover, and cook 15 minutes. Add the chilies, green onions and cilantro. Reduce the heat and simmer 5 minutes. Add salt and pepper to taste.

Serves 12

JOHN JACOB'S
EL PARADOR
Tucson
Chef Consuelo Flores

CREAM OF JALAPEÑO SOUP

3/4C Celery, diced
3/4C Carrots, diced
3/4C Bell Pepper, diced
2C Chicken Stock
10T Butter
1C Onions, diced
3/4C Flour
4C Chicken Stock
2C Swiss Cheese, shredded
2C Cheddar Cheese, shredded
3 Jalapeños, seeded and diced
1/8t Nutmeg
Salt, to taste
1 qt. Whipping Cream, hot

Garnish:
Popcorn or hot Tortilla Strips

Simmer 10 minutes:
Place the celery, carrots, bell pepper, and chicken stock in a 1 or 2 qt. saucepan. Bring to a boil, Reduce heat and simmer until tender, about 10 minutes. Set the saucepan aside. Do not drain.

Heat 25 to 35 minutes:
In a 4 or 5 quart saucepan, melt the butter over medium heat. Add the onions and saute until translucent. Add the flour and cook 5 to 7 minutes, stirring continuously. Do not brown. Turn the heat to low and slowly stir in the chicken stock. Whisk constantly until the sauce thickens. Blend in the Swiss and cheddar cheese. Stir until melted. Add the undrained vegetables, jalapeños, nutmeg, and salt. Cook 15 to 20 minutes. Just before serving, stir in hot whipping cream.

Serve:
Garnish with popcorn or crisp tortilla strips.

Serves 6

ENCHANTMENT RESORT
Sedona
Chef Gerald Peters

CREAMY SWEET POTATO JALAPEÑO SOUP

4 lbs. Sweet Potatoes (3 very large)
4C Milk
1C Cream
2T Olive Oil
1C Onion, finely diced
2t fresh Garlic
1t Thyme, dried
1t Basil, dried
1C Celery, finely diced
1C Zucchini, finely diced
1C Cauliflower, finely diced
1C Water
1 to 2t Jalapeños, diced
1T Parsley, dried
1T Sherry
1T Soy Sauce
1t White Pepper

Garnish:
1/2C Sour Cream
1-1/2T Lime Juice

Bake 40 to 50 minutes:
Prick the potatoes and bake at 350 degrees until soft. When they are done and cool, pull off the skins.

Puree:
Puree the sweet potatoes, milk, and cream. Set aside.

Saute and simmer several minutes:
Saute the onion, garlic, thyme, and basil in oil until the onion is translucent. Add the celery, zucchini, cauliflower, and water. Simmer until tender.

Simmer 1 hour:
Place the sweet potato puree and sauteed vegetables in a large soup pot. Add the jalapeños, parsley, sherry, soy sauce, and white pepper. Simmer 1 hour over low heat.

Serve:
The soup can be served immediately, or you can let the flavors develop more fully overnight. It can be served hot or cold. If you desire a garnish, mix the sour cream and lime juice. Add 2T to each bowl of soup, and swirl with a spoon.

Serves 6

MACY'S
EUROPEAN COFFEEHOUSE
AND BAKERY
Flagstaff
Chef Sue-Bug Skelton

CREAM OF MUSHROOM SOUP

2-1/2C Mushrooms
3/4C Onion, chopped
3/4C Butter
3/4C Flour
1-1/2 qts. Chicken Broth
2 cans Evaporated Milk
3/4t White Pepper
1/2t Seasoned Salt

Saute:
Saute the mushrooms and onions in butter over medium heat for 5 minutes. Blend in the flour. Cook and stir until slightly thickened.

Heat 20 to 35 minutes:
Place the chicken broth, evaporated milk, white pepper, and seasoned salt in a double boiler. Heat over a medium flame until the broth thickens, 15 to 30 minutes. Add the mushroom mixture to the broth and heat until thickened.

Serves 10 to 12

MOLLY BUTLER LODGE
Greer
Chef Stephen R. Cooksley

SWISS ONION SOUP

1 large Onion, sliced
1T Butter
1/2t Salt
1t fresh ground Pepper
1 pinch Nutmeg
4C Beef Stock
4 slices Sour Dough Bread, toasted
4 thin slices Swiss Cheese

Heat several minutes:
Saute the onion in butter until translucent. Add salt, pepper, nutmeg, and beef stock. Bring to a boil.

Broil:
Pour the soup into 4 bowls and top each with a slice of bread and cheese. Broil until golden brown.

Serves 4

CHEZ RENE'S
SWISS CHALET
Wickenburg
Chef Rene Lenggenhager

LEEK BISQUE

1/2C Butter
12 medium Leeks, thinly sliced, keeping white
   bulbs and tender part of green
2 medium Carrots, thinly sliced
2 cloves Garlic, minced
3/4C Parsley, chopped
2t Lemon Peel, grated
2t Marjoram
1/8t White Pepper
1/2C Flour
8C Milk, warm
Chicken Broth, to taste

Garnish:
Toasted Almonds, sliced
Crisp cooked Bacon, crumbled
Croutons or thinly sliced Leek Stems

Heat 25 to 30 minutes:
Melt the butter over medium heat. Add the leeks, carrots, garlic,
parsley, lemon peel, marjoram, and white pepper. Saute until the
vegetables are tender. Stir in the flour and cook 5 to 10 minutes.
Add the milk and heat until steaming. Add the chicken broth and
heat until steaming.

Serve:
Serve with toasted almonds, cooked bacon, and croutons or thinly
sliced leek stems.

Serves 8 to 10

**MOLLY BUTLER
LODGE**
Greer
Chef Stephen R. Cooksley

BRANDIED ONION BISQUE

1/2 lb. Butter *
2 medium Onions, sliced
1/4C Brandy
1/4C Sherry
1t Tarragon
2t Garlic Salt
4C Beef Stock
3C Heavy Cream

*This soup is extremely flavorful and rich. If you prefer a lighter soup, use less butter.

Heat 30 minutes:
In a one gallon pot, melt the butter over medium heat. Add the onions and saute 5 minutes until translucent. Add the brandy, sherry, tarragon, and garlic salt. Reduce 3 to 4 minutes. Add the beef stock and bring to a boil, stirring occasionally. Remove from heat and allow to cool. Add the cream and bring to a boil. Reduce the heat and simmer 15 minutes.

Serve:
Serve hot, garnished with chopped green onions.

Serves 8

THE IMPECCABLE PIG
Scottsdale
Chef Shane Taggart

BEEF & VEAL

Steak Tartare

Steak Scordato

Mesquite-Grilled Black Angus Beef with
Black Bean Salsa

Southwestern Filet

Navajo Taco

El Charro Carne Verde

Ropa Vieja

Chili

Meatloaf on Potato Pancakes with
Chipotle Ketchup

Pot Roast

Ossobuco Avanti

Scallopini Stresa

Veal Regina

Beef and Veal Medallion Duet

Sauteed Veal Boursin Quesadillas in Masa
with Tomatillo Chipotle Salsa

STEAK TARTARE

For a lively twist on this classic preparation, raw tuna may be substituted for beef.

4 Anchovy filets
1/8T Dry Mustard
1/4T Red Wine Vinegar
1T Garlic Oil
2 dashes of Tabasco Sauce
2 dashes of Worcestershire Sauce
1 Egg Yolk, raw
6 oz. raw Sirloin or Tenderloin, finely chopped
1T Onion, minced
1T fresh Parsley, chopped
1 Hard Cooked Egg, grated
1 dash of Cognac or Brandy, optional
Salt and freshly ground Pepper to taste
2T Capers, whole

Garnish:
Romaine Lettuce
Tomatoes
Rye Bread, French Bread, or Sourdough Toast

Mix:
In a wooden bowl, use 2 forks to crush the anchovies to a paste. Add the mustard, vinegar, oil, tabasco, and Worcestershire. Blend thoroughly. Add the egg yolk and mix. Add the beef and mix. Add the onion, parsley, hard cooked egg, cognac, salt, and pepper. Mix well. Add the capers and mix lightly. Be careful not to crush the capers.

Serve:
Place the mixture on Romaine lettuce leaves and garnish with sliced tomatoes. Serve with rye, French bread, or sourdough toast.

 **THE TACK ROOM**
Tucson
The Kane and Vactor Family

Serves 2

STEAK SCORDATO

This recipe came from Sicily with the Scordato family around the turn of the century. A distant relative who ate Steak Scordato at our restaurant commented how similar it was to his own mother's recipe over 50 years ago.

4 pieces of Steak, 12 to 14 oz. each
2C Bread Crumbs
1/3C Romano Cheese, freshly ground
2/3t Salt
2/3t Pepper
2/3t Garlic Powder
2t Oregano
2t Parsley, dried
Clarified Butter, melted
Olive Oil

Tenderloin or New York Strip Sirloin are the preferred cuts for this recipe, although you can use any steak.

Mix:
Mix the bread crumbs and seasonings.

Coat:
Coat the entire steak with olive oil and then bread crumbs. Pat the crumbs on to help them stick. Drizzle butter on top.

Broil:
Cook the steaks on a flat pan under a broiler. Turn when lightly brown, adding more bread crumbs and butter if needed. Cook to desired stage. Mr. Scordato recommends rare to medium.

Serves 4

SCORDATO'S RESTAURANT
Tucson
Chef Jim Scordato

MESQUITE-GRILLED BLACK ANGUS BEEF WITH BLACK BEAN SALSA

2-1/2 lbs. Flank Steak, trimmed
2 large cloves Garlic, crushed
2T Olive Oil
1T mild Chili Powder
1/2t Cumin, ground

Garnish:
Black Bean Salsa, recipe follows

Coat:
In a small bowl, blend the garlic, oil, chili powder, and cumin. With a sharp knife, score one side of the meat lightly at one-inch intervals. Rub the seasonings into both sides of the meat. Sprinkle both sides with salt. Wrap tightly in plastic wrap.

Refrigerate overnight.

Grill:
Grill to desired doneness over mesquite charcoal.

Serve:
Serve with Black Bean Salsa.

Serves 6

BLACK BEAN SALSA

4C Black Beans
2 Tomatoes, peeled and seeded
1C Red Onion, diced
1/2C Bell Pepper, diced
1/4C Jalapeño Pepper, finely diced
1/2t Cumin Powder
1/2t Chili Powder
1/2t Ginger Powder
1T Garlic, chopped
Zest and juice of 2 Lemons
Zest and juice of 1 Orange
Salt and Pepper to taste

Soak overnight and simmer 2 hours:
Soak the beans in warm water overnight. Then simmer in fresh water
2 hours until tender. Rinse well and drain.

Mix:
In a bowl, lightly toss the beans with the remaining ingredients.

Chill.

Serve:
Black Bean Salsa goes well with Black Angus Beef and other meats
or seafood.

Serves 6 to 10

ENCHANTMENT
RESORT
Sedona
Chef Gerald Peters

SOUTHWESTERN FILET

1/4C Mushrooms, diced
1/4C Green Bell Pepper, diced
1/4C Onions, diced
2T Green Chili, diced
6 Filet Mignons, 8 oz. each
1/2C Monterey Jack Cheese, grated

Saute 3 to 4 minutes:
Saute the mushrooms, green bell pepper, onions and green chili in oil. Cool.

Stuff:
Slit a pocket almost all the way through each filet. Stuff 1/3 of each pocket with grated cheese, 1/3 with the vegetable mixture, the last third with more cheese. Pin the pockets closed with toothpicks.

Grill few minutes (optional):
Place the filets on a hot grill, just long enough to sear grill marks. Flip over and repeat.

Bake 10 to 15 minutes:
Bake at 400 degrees.

Serves 6

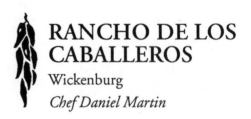

RANCHO DE LOS CABALLEROS
Wickenburg
Chef Daniel Martin

NAVAJO TACO

2-1/3C Pinto Beans
1 lb. Ground Beef
3T Chili Powder
1T Cumin
Dash of Salt
2C Chopped Onions
1 can Tomato Puree, 6 oz.
Fry Bread, recipe p. 29
Shredded Cheese
Shredded Lettuce
Chopped Tomatoes
Salsa, if desired

Soak overnight and simmer 2 to 3 hours:
Soak the pinto beans overnight in warm water. Place the soaked
beans in enough fresh water to keep the beans covered, and simmer
until tender.

Saute and simmer 35 to 40 minutes:
Saute the beef in a skillet over medium heat. Drain any excess fat. In
a bowl, mix the chili powder, cumin, and salt. Add them to the
skillet, along with the cooked beans, onions, and tomato puree. If
you prefer a thinner sauce, add water. Bring the mixture to a boil,
reduce the heat and simmer 30 minutes.

Serve:
Spoon the beef mixture onto Fry Bread. Top with cheese, lettuce,
tomatoes, and salsa.

Serves 4

NAVAJO CAFE
Navajo
Chef Sarah Spencer

EL CHARRO
CARNE VERDE
Green Chile and Beef Stew

The meat and vegetables can be prepared early and refrigerated until you are ready to finish the stew.

> 3 lbs. Roast of Beef *
> 3 qts. Water
> 1 medium White Onion, quartered
> 1T Salt, or to taste
> 1T Pepper
> 2 large Potatoes, peeled and cubed
> 8 Green Chilies
> 1/2C Oil
> 1 medium White Onion, sliced
> 1/4C Garlic Puree
> 2T Flour
> 2 large Tomatoes, cubed

> *Eye round, brisket, or chuck beef will work
> fine for this recipe.

PREPARATION

Simmer 2 hours:
Bring 3 qts. water to boil in an 8 quart stock pot. Add the roast, quartered onion, salt, and pepper. Bring the broth to a boil again and skim off any froth. Lower the heat and simmer until the meat is tender, removing froth frequently.

Boil:
Boil the potatoes until they are done.

Roast, peel and dice:
Roast, peel and dice the chilies.

Reserve:

When the meat is tender, remove it and cut into 1/2 inch pieces, trimming any gristle and most of the fat. Set aside. Reserve 1 cup of broth for later use in this recipe. The remaining sauce may be used as beef stock in other recipes.

THE STEW

Saute and simmer 15 minutes:
In a large skillet, saute the onion slices in oil over medium heat. Cook until the onion is soft, but not brown. Stir in the meat, a little at a time. Add the garlic puree and simmer over low heat for a few minutes until the garlic is well mixed.

Dissolve the flour in a small amount of reserved broth. Then combine it with remaining cup of broth and add it to the skillet. Simmer for a few minutes until the sauce thickens. Gently fold in the chilies, potatoes, and tomatoes. Simmer until just bubbling. Taste and adjust seasonings.

Serves 6 to 8

EL CHARRO
Tucson
Chef Carlotta Flores

ROPA VIEJA

"Ropa Vieja" means old clothes. The name was given to this Cuban dish because the meat falls apart in shreds (like old clothes) after cooking. Because meat was very expensive, recipes such as this were often invented to make it go farther.

2 to 2-1/2 lbs. Flank Steak or Beef Brisket,
  well trimmed of fat
1 Onion, whole
2 Garlic Cloves, whole
1 Bay Leaf
2t Salt
1/2t Pepper
2C Water

1/3C Olive Oil
1 large Onion, thinly sliced
1 large Green Bell Pepper, julienne
1 large Red Bell Pepper, julienne
3 large Garlic Cloves, minced
1 can Tomatoes, 16 oz., coarsely chopped
  with liquid
1/2C Dry Red Wine
1-1/2t Salt
1t Cumin, ground
1t Oregano, dried
1 large Bay Leaf

2C Long Grain White Rice
3C Water
2t Salt
1T Butter

Simmer 2 hours:
Place the beef, 1 onion, 2 garlic cloves, 1 bay leaf, salt, and pepper in a large saucepan with enough water to cover all the ingredients.

Bring to a boil, reduce heat and simmer until meat becomes very tender.

Remove beef from the broth. Shred the meat by pulling it apart with your hands. Remove the bay leaf and reserve 1C of the broth.

Saute and simmer 25 to 30 minutes:
Heat 1/3C oil in a large skillet over medium high heat. Add 1 onion, the green bell pepper, red bell pepper, and garlic, and cook until tender. Add the shredded beef, reserved broth, tomatoes with liquid, wine, salt, cumin, oregano, and 1 bay leaf. Lower the heat to medium and cook covered, stirring occasionally. Cook until the liquid is reduced by half, about 20 minutes.

Cook 20 minutes:
Cook the rice, salt, and butter in water until tender.

Serve:
Remove the bay leaf. Ladle the meat and vegetables on top of the rice.

Serves 6

HAVANA CAFE
Phoenix
The Hernandez Family

CHILI

1 lb. Ground Beef
1 small Onion
20 oz. Kidney Beans, canned
40 oz. Crushed Tomatoes, canned
10 oz. Tomato Puree, canned
9 oz. Tomato Juice
5T Chili Powder
1T Garlic Powder
2 medium Jalapeños, finely chopped
Salt and Pepper to taste
Pinch of Oregano, dried
Pinch of Thyme, dried
1C Cheddar Cheese, grated

Saute and simmer 1 hour:
Brown the beef and onion over medium heat. Drain off excess fat.
Add the beans, tomatoes, tomato puree, tomato juice, chili powder,
garlic powder, jalapeños, salt, pepper, oregano, and thyme. Bring to
a boil, reduce heat to low, and simmer 45 to 60 minutes, stirring
occasionally.

Serve:
Serve topped with cheddar cheese.

Serves 6 to 8

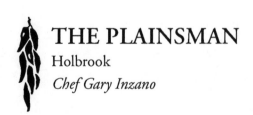

THE PLAINSMAN
Holbrook
Chef Gary Inzano

MEATLOAF ON POTATO PANCAKES WITH CHIPOTLE KETCHUP

MEATLOAF

3/4C Onions, finely diced
1/2C Carrots, finely diced
1/4C Celery, finely diced
1/4C Red Bell Pepper, finely diced
1/4C Green Bell Pepper, finely diced
3t Garlic, finely minced
1/2C Tomato Ketchup
1/2C Half and Half
3 Eggs, well beaten
2 lbs. Ground Beef
3/4 lbs. Chorizo Sausage
3/4C Bread Crumbs
Salt and Black Pepper, to taste
Potato Pancakes, recipe follows
Chipotle Ketchup, recipe follows

Saute:
Saute the onions, carrots, celery, bell peppers, and garlic until the vegetables are soft. Cool.

Knead:
In a bowl, blend the ketchup, half and half, and eggs. Add the sauteed vegetables, beef, sausage, bread crumbs, salt, and pepper. Knead 5 minutes.

Bake 50 minutes:
Lightly pack the meatloaf into a greased loaf pan. Set the loaf pan in a larger pan. Add water to the larger pan until the water level reaches half the height of the loaf pan. Bake at 375 degrees.

(continued on next page)

Let stand 20 minutes:
Remove the meatloaf from the oven and let it stand before removing it from the pan.

Serve:
Spread Chipotle Ketchup on a pancake. Add a slice of meatloaf, more Chipotle Ketchup, and another pancake. Cut the pancake edges to form a square, then cut through at a diagonal, as you would a sandwich.

Serves 8

POTATO PANCAKES

> 8 Potatoes, grated
> 2 small Onions, grated
> 4 Eggs
> 1/3C all-purpose Flour
> 3/4t Baking Powder
> 1/4C Cilantro, chopped
> Salt and Pepper, to taste

Rinse 10 minutes:
Rinse the potatoes with cold, running water until all the brown is gone. Place in a cloth and squeeze out any excess water.

Mix:
Mix the potatoes, onions, eggs, flour, baking powder, cilantro, salt, and pepper.

Fry:
Spoon the potato mixture onto a greased griddle or fry pan. Flatten to desired thickness. Cook until golden brown on one side. Turn the pancake over and brown the other side.

CHIPOTLE KETCHUP

1C Tomato Ketchup
1 Chipotle Chili, canned

Puree:
Puree the ketchup and chili. For a spicier ketchup, add more
chipotle. If you prefer a milder flavor, use more ketchup.

THE PHOENICIAN
WINDOWS ON THE GREEN
Scottsdale
Chef Lenard Rubin

POT ROAST

1/2C Salad Oil
1/2t Thyme, dried
1/2t Black Pepper
1 clove Garlic, crushed
5 lbs. Chuck, bottom, round or shoulder
2 qts. Beef Stock
2 Carrots, diced
2 Onions, medium diced
1 Bay leaf

Coat:
Mix the salad oil, thyme, pepper and garlic. Rub the mixture on the chuck.

Bake 3 hours-20 minutes:
In a heavy pot, bake the meat 20 minutes at 400 degrees until lightly browned. Add the stock, carrots, onion, and bay leaf. Cover the pot tightly and bake 3 hours at 375 degrees until the beef is tender.

Serves 15

BROWN GRAVY

Broth from pot roast, strained, hot
1/2C Flour
8T Butter, melted

Roux:
Heat the butter until very hot. With a fork, stir flour into the butter. Whisk until smooth and heat several minutes. Slowly stir the roux into the hot broth with a wire whip until your desired consistency is reached.

Simmer 15 minutes:
Lightly simmer the sauce. If it becomes too thick, add more beef stock.

THE LANDMARK RESTAURANT
Mesa
Chef Eric Foust

OSSOBUCO AVANTI

6 Veal Shanks, 5 inches long
1C Flour
1/2C Olive Oil
1C White Wine
2 Carrots, chopped coarsely
2 large Onions, chopped coarsely
3 Celery stalks, chopped coarsely
2C Tomato Puree
Salt and Pepper, to taste
Water

Coat:
Wash and dry the veal. Coat with flour.

Saute and simmer:
Saute the veal in hot olive oil until brown on all sides. Add white wine and cook until evaporated. Add the carrots, onions, and celery stalks. Simmer until nicely roasted and dark brown. Add the tomato puree, salt, and pepper and cook until heated.

Bake several hours:
Place the meat and vegetables in a roasting pan just large enough to hold the ingredients. Cover with water. Bake at 300 degrees until tender. When the meat is done, check the sauce consistency. If it needs to be thickened, add a little cornstarch diluted in water and heat until your desired consistency is reached.

Serves 6

AVANTI
Phoenix, Scottsdale
Chef Raul Peña

SCALLOPINI STRESA

4 slices Mozarella Cheese
4 very thin slices Prosciutto Ham
8 Veal Cutlets, 3 oz. each
2 Eggs, beaten
1C Milk
1C Flour
2C Seasoned Bread Crumbs
Olive Oil, to coat pan
1T Marsala Wine
1/2C White Wine
1C Veal Stock, slightly thickened

Wrap the cheese and ham:
Fold 1 piece of cheese around each piece of ham. Lay 2 pieces of
veal in the form of an "X". Set 1 folded piece of cheese and ham in
the middle of the "X" and fold the veal ends over to enclose.

Coat:
Mix the eggs and milk. Dredge the folded veal in flour, then in the
egg-milk mixture, and then in bread crumbs.

Saute and simmer 20 to 25 minutes:
Place the coated veal in a hot pan coated with olive oil. Reduce the
heat to low and saute 15 to 20 minutes. Drain the oil. Add the
Marsala and white wine and reduce by half. Add the veal stock and
simmer 2 minutes until thickened.

Serves 4

**SCORDATO'S
RESTAURANT**
Tucson
Chef Jim Scordato

VEAL REGINA

4T Flour
1/2t Salt
1/4t White Pepper
8 Veal Loin Medallions, 3 oz. each
1T Butter
1t Oil
1/2 Red Onion, sliced
4 large Mushrooms, sliced
6 Sun Dried Tomatoes, julienne (1/4C)
1/8C Pistachio Nuts
1/2C Dry Marsala Wine
1C Veal Stock
1T Pesto
1/2t Salt
1/4t White Pepper

Garnish:
Sprigs of Basil

Coat:
Dredge the veal in a mixture of flour, salt, and 1/4t white pepper.

Saute and simmer 25 minutes:
Saute the veal in butter and oil until golden brown. Remove the veal from the pan. In the same pan, saute the onion, mushrooms, tomatoes, and nuts. Deglaze with wine. Add the stock, pesto, salt, and 1/4t white pepper, and simmer 5 minutes. Add the sauteed veal and simmer 5 more minutes.

Serve:
Divide the veal among 4 plates and spoon sauce on top. Garnish with sprigs of basil, if desired.

Serves 4

COTTAGE PLACE
Flagstaff
Chef Kurt Gottschalk

BEEF AND VEAL MEDALLION DUET

A somewhat complicated preparation, the ensuing presentation is worth the work!

> **2 lbs. Beef Tenderloin**
> **Salt and Pepper, to taste**
> **2T Shallots, finely chopped**
> **1t Garlic, finely chopped**
> **3 lbs. Spinach, stems removed**
> **Pinch of Salt**
> **Pinch of Pepper**
> **2 lbs. Veal Top Round, cut into 6 slices**
> **1 bunch Basil, finely chopped (1/8C after chopping)**
> **1 bunch fresh Tarragon, finely chopped (1/8C)**
> **Pinch of Salt**
> **Pinch of Pepper**
> **Madeira Glaze, recipe follows**

Sear:
Cut the beef into strips 1 inch wide and 3 inches long. Sear lightly on all sides, and season with salt and pepper. Cool.

Saute:
Saute the shallots and garlic in a skillet over medium heat until the shallots become translucent. Add the spinach and a pinch of salt and pepper. Saute over high heat until bright green. Cool.

Season:
Lightly pound the veal. Season with basil, tarragon, salt, and pepper.

Form rolls:
Lay a piece of veal on a sheet of caul fat or butcher twine. Spoon on some spinach mixture, and top with a piece of tenderloin. Roll the veal and spinach around the tenderloin. Encase each roll with caul fat or tie with butcher twine.

Bake 15 minutes:
Roast the rolls in a roasting pan at 450 degrees. Adjust the roasting time for the thickness of the rolls. Mr. Biggs recommends this dish be served medium rare.

Rest 5 minutes:
Remove the rolls from the oven and allow to rest.

Serve:
Slice each roll into 3 pieces and serve topped with Madeira Glaze.

Serves 10 - 12

MADEIRA GLAZE

> 2T Shallots, finely chopped
> 1t fresh Thyme Leaves, without stems
> 2C Madeira
> 3C Veal Demi-Glaze
> 1C Madeira
> Salt and Pepper, to taste
> Arrowroot, as needed

Saute and simmer 25 to 30 minutes:
Saute the shallots in a skillet until lightly browned. Add the thyme and 2C Madeira. Reduce by 2/3. Add the demi-glaze and reduce by half. Add 1C Madeira, salt, and pepper. Thicken with arrowroot, as needed.

WESTCOURT IN
THE BUTTES
TOP OF THE ROCK
Tempe
Chef Franklin Biggs

SAUTEED VEAL BOURSIN QUESADILLAS IN MASA WITH TOMATILLO CHIPOTLE SALSA

8 oz. Veal Stew Meat, cut into thin slices
1 Red Onion, sliced thin
1 Green Jalapeño, diced
1 bunch Cilantro, chopped
1/4t Salt
2C Water
4 oz. Boursin Cheese*, in small pieces
1C Masa Flour
1C White Flour
1/2C Pompeian Olive Oil
1/4t ground Black Pepper
2t Salt
Tomato Chipotle Salsa, recipe follows

*Boursin cheese is a cream cheese seasoned with pepper, parsley, and garlic.

Simmer 30 minutes:
Gently simmer the veal, onion, jalapeño, cilantro, and salt with water, covered. Drain. When cool, add the cheese.

Blend:
In a food processor, mix the flours, oil, pepper, and salt. Blend until the dough takes the shape of a large ball.

Form quesadillas:
Divide the dough into four rounds. Roll into tortillas 1/8 inch thick, and 5 inches in diameter. Add the veal mixture. Fold into semicircles, making sure the edges stick.

Fry:
Fry the quesadillas gently in oil until browned on both sides. When done, blot any excess oil with a paper towel.

Serve:
Set the quesadillas on a bed of Tomatillo Chipotle Salsa.

Serves 4

TOMATILLO CHIPOTLE SALSA

4 Tomatilloes
1 clove Garlic
1 Chipotle Chili
1/4 bunch Cilantro
2T Pompeian Olive Oil
1t Chicken Base
1/4t Kosher Salt
Pinch of Black Pepper
1 Tomato, diced

Mix:
Blend all the ingredients except the diced tomato until smooth.
Adjust the seasonings. Fold in the tomato.

INN AT
McCORMICK RANCH
PIÑON GRILL
Scottsdale
Chef Farn Boggie

LAMB, PORK & VENISON

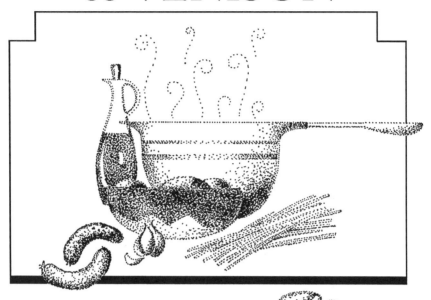

Lamb Chop with Onion Mint Marmalade
Barbecued Leg of Lamb
Lamb with Spring Vegetables
Mutton Stew
Penne with Sausage and Peppered Vodka Sauce
Sausage a la Raffaele
Nam Sod
El Tovar Chili
Roast Iowa Pork Tenderloin with
　Sage and Cider Sauce
Pork Chops with Apple Cornbread Stuffing
Black Bean and Venison Chili

LAMB CHOP WITH ONION MINT MARMALADE

1 rack of Lamb, frenched
8T Olive Oil
2t Jalapeño Honey Mustard*
1C Pistachios, chopped
2T Shallots, finely chopped
4T Tomatoes, finely chopped
1/2C Red Wine
1/2C Demi Glaze
2t Mint Leaves, finely chopped
1t fresh Oregano, chopped
1t fresh Thyme, chopped
2 Baby Leeks, grilled or sauteed
Salt and Pepper to taste

Garnish:
Onion Mint Marmalade, recipe follows
Fresh Seasonal Vegetables
Mint

*Jalapeño Honey Mustard can be purchased in
Southwest supply markets (see appendix).

Sear:
In a heavy skillet, sear the lamb in olive oil. Cook until golden
brown on both sides. Cool slightly.

Coat:
Glaze the lamb with jalapeño honey mustard. Roll in pistachios.

Bake 12 to 15 minutes:
Bake at 350 degrees.

Saute and simmer 12 to 15 minutes:
Using same skillet, saute the shallots until golden brown. Add the tomatoes and simmer 1 minute. Add the wine and cook until the liquid is reduced by half. Add the demi glaze, mint, oregano, thyme, leeks, salt, and pepper. Saute 3 to 4 minutes.

Serve:
Pour the sauce on a preheated dinner plate, and place the lamb on top. Garnish with Onion Mint Marmalade, leek, and fresh seasonal vegetables.

Serves 2

ONION MINT MARMALADE

> 1/4C Olive Oil
> 1C Red Onions, sliced
> 1C Pearl Onions, peeled
> 1/2C Sugar
> 1/2C Demi Glaze
> 1/2C fresh Mint Leaves, chopped

Saute and simmer:
Heat a skillet over medium-high flame. Add the oil, red onions and pearl onions. Saute until lightly browned. Lower the heat to medium. Add the sugar and demi glaze, and reduce the liquid by half.

Add:
Let the sauce cool to room temperature and add the mint.

Serves 10 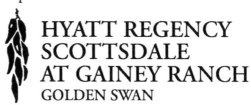 HYATT REGENCY
SCOTTSDALE
AT GAINEY RANCH
GOLDEN SWAN

Scottsdale

Chef Anton Brunbauer

BARBECUED
LEG OF LAMB

Barbecued Leg of Lamb is one of Mr. Colon's favorite
summer recipes.

Lamb:
7 lb. Leg of Lamb, boned and separated into parts

Marinade:
1/2 medium Onion, chopped
1/2C fresh Cilantro
1 inch cube fresh Ginger, chopped
1T Coriander Seeds, toasted in dry skillet for 5
    minutes and crushed
2 cloves Garlic, halved
1t Black Pepper Corns, crushed
2T Sea Salt
1/2C Lemon Juice, strained
1/4C Olive Oil

Sauce:
3 Tomatoes, large, cored, and coarsely chopped
1C Dry White Wine
3T Imported Dijon Mustard
Kosher Salt
Freshly ground Black Pepper
1/4 lb. Lightly Salted Butter, cut into small pieces.

Garnish:
See serving suggestions below.

Refrigerate 2 days:
In a bowl, mix all the marinade ingredients. Place the lamb in a glass
dish and spread the marinade on top. Cover and refrigerate, turning
once or twice.

When done, remove the lamb and save the marinade. 1/4C marinade will be used in the sauce; the remaining marinade will be used when grilling the lamb.

Simmer 20 minutes:
In a heavy saucepan, combine the tomatoes and wine. Bring to a boil, then reduce heat and simmer until the mixture becomes thick.

Combine:
Mix the tomato mixture and 1/4C reserved marinade. Rub it through a fine strainer into a heat-proof bowl. Set aside.

Grill 20 minutes:
Wipe the lamb dry and set it on a grill over hot coals. Baste with the remaining reserved marinade, and turn after 10 minutes. Cook 10 minutes on the other side. The lamb will be rare.

Marinate 5 minutes:
Roll the lamb in the remaining marinade and let it rest 5 minutes before slicing.

Heat:
Beat the reserved tomato-marinade mixture with mustard in the heat-proof bowl. Add salt and pepper. Set the bowl over boiling water until it becomes hot. Add the butter by beating the pieces in, bit by bit.

Serve:
Serve the tomato-marinade sauce with the lamb. Since the lamb dish comes with its own sauce, which is virtually a vegetable, you will, at most, want some rice or good bread to serve with it. The lamb might well be preceded by a light soup or a fresh vegetable, and followed, if you are cooking outdoors in the summer, by a fruit compote or sorbet.

Serves 8

EL TOVAR
Grand Canyon
Chef Esteban Colon

LAMB WITH SPRING VEGETABLES

3T Butter
4 cloves Garlic, minced
3 lbs. Lamb, boneless shoulder or leg,
   cut in small pieces
1T dried Thyme
1/4C Flour
3 to 4 Tomatoes, peeled, seeded, and
   chopped (1-1/2C)
1/2C Carrots, chopped
2C Chicken Stock
1/2 lb. fresh Green Beans, snipped
1 lb. fresh Asparagus
1/2 lb. fresh Pea Pods, snipped
12 Green Onions, white bulb and a little green
Salt and Pepper, to taste

Saute and simmer 2 hours:
Saute the garlic in butter over medium high heat. Add the lamb and thyme. Stir and brown. Sprinkle flour onto the browned meat, and stir until all the flour is absorbed. Add the tomatoes, carrots, and stock. Simmer covered 1-3/4 to 2 hours. Do not boil. When done, remove the lamb and place it on a heated serving platter.

Boil 15 minutes:
Add the beans, asparagus, pea pods, and green onions to the broth. Boil 3 to 5 minutes, until tender. Remove the vegetables and place them on the serving platter. Continue boiling until the broth is slightly thickened, about 10 minutes. Season with salt and pepper.

Serve:
Pour the broth over the lamb and serve immediately.

Serves 6

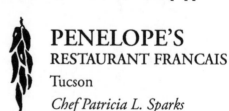

PENELOPE'S
RESTAURANT FRANCAIS
Tucson
Chef Patricia L. Sparks

MUTTON STEW

2-1/2 lbs. Mutton, diced
2T Margarine
2C Carrots
3/4C Yellow Onions, chopped medium
2C Celery, 1/4 inch slices
3 Medium Potatoes, chopped
1/2T Salt
1/2T Black Pepper
12C Water

Brown:
In a stock pot, brown the mutton in margarine. When done, drain in a colander. Set the mutton aside.

Simmer 2 hours:
Place the remaining ingredients in the same pot. Bring the broth to a boil, reduce the heat to low, and simmer until the carrots and potatoes are tender, about 1-1/2 hours. Add the mutton and simmer 15 minutes.

Serves 16

NAVAJO NATION INN
Window Rock
Chef Regis Tsosie

PENNE WITH SAUSAGE AND PEPPERED VODKA SAUCE

6 oz. dried Penne*
1T Olive Oil, heated
6 oz. Hot Italian Sausage, ground
   or removed from casings
1 clove Garlic, crushed
4T Peppered Vodka, such as Absolut
3/4C Tomato Sauce, any light tomato sauce
8 medium Black Pitted Olives, cut in half
2 large fresh Basil Leaves
Salt to taste
1/2C Fontina Cheese, shredded or thinly sliced

*Penne is a tubular pasta, also known as pencil point pasta.

Boil 8 to 11 minutes:
Boil the penne in 3 quarts water. Cook one minute less than normal,
al dente.

Heat 18 minutes:
Over medium heat, saute the sausage in oil until the sausage is well
browned, about 10 minutes. Add the garlic, and stir for a few seconds.
Carefully pour the vodka over the meat (watch your hands and face as
it ignites). When the flames subside, reduce the heat to low and add
the tomato sauce, olives, basil, and salt. Simmer 5 minutes.

Bake 15 minutes:
Drain the pasta and mix it gently with the sauce. Place the mixture in
a buttered baking dish. Sprinkle with fontina. Bake at 375 degrees.

Serves 2

DANIEL'S
Tucson
Chef Daniel Scordato

SAUSAGE A LA RAFFAELE

1 lb. Fettucini, imported
8 links Mild Italian Sausage
2T Olive Oil
2 cloves Garlic
1/2C Leek, sliced (1 fresh leek)
1/2 lb. mixture of fresh Mushrooms*
1/2C White Wine
1-1/2C Veal or Beef Stock
2T Butter
Salt and Pepper, to taste

*Oyster, Shiitake and Porcini mushrooms are ideal
choices for this recipe.

Boil:
Boil the fettucini in lightly salted water.

Cook:
Barbeque the sausage. If a barbecue is not convenient, cooking on the
stove top is fine. When done, cut 4 of the links into slices, and leave
the other links whole.

Saute and simmer 15 to 20 minutes:
In a saucepan, saute the garlic in oil over medium-low heat. Cook
until golden brown. Add the leek and cook until translucent. Add the
mushrooms and cooked sausage, and saute 5 to 10 minutes. Add the
wine, bring to a boil, and reduce slightly. Add the stock, butter, salt,
and pepper. Reduce slightly.

Serve:
Arrange the sausage and mushrooms
on top of the fettucini.

Serves 4

RAFFAELE'S
Phoenix
Chef Raffaele Contacessi

NAM SOD

1C Ground Pork
3T Water
1 to 1-1/2T Fish Sauce
1 to 1-1/2T Lemon Juice
1/2t Ground Red Chili Pepper
1T Green Onion, chopped
1/2T Cilantro, chopped
1/2T Ginger, shredded
1T Red Onion, sliced
1T Unsalted Roasted Peanuts

Garnish:
1/2 head Iceberg Lettuce

Saute 5 to 7 minutes:
In a small skillet, over a hot flame, cook the pork with 3T water (just enough water to keep the pork from sticking, but do not boil). Saute until the pork is cooked. Drain.

Mix:
In a bowl, mix the pork and remaining ingredients well.

Serve:
Arrange the lettuce on a platter. Place the pork and dressing on the lettuce.

Serves 2

**PINK PEPPER
THAI CUISINE**
Scottsdale, Mesa, Phoenix
Chef Tony Tavee

EL TOVAR CHILI

El Tovar Chili won every chili contest entered!

- 1-1/2 lbs. Tomatoes, (4 to 6 tomatoes) peeled and coarsely chopped*
- 3/4t Salt
- 1/4t Pepper, freshly ground
- 1-1/2 lbs. Sirloin, chopped
- 1-1/2 lbs. Pork, diced
- 1 large Onion, chopped
- 3 large cloves Garlic, minced
- 3C Beer
- 8 oz. Tomato Sauce
- 1/2C Chili Powder
- 1T Salt
- 1t Paprika
- 1t Cayenne Pepper
- 2t Instant Masa Harina
- 3T Water

*If fresh, in season tomatoes are not available, use canned.

Simmer 10 minutes:
Cook the tomatoes, salt, and pepper over medium heat until a thick, rich sauce forms. You will use 1C below; the remainder can be used in other dishes.

Saute and simmer 3 hours-45 minutes:
Place the sirloin, pork, onion, and garlic in a large, heavy saucepan over medium heat. Cook, stirring until the meat is no longer pink. Mix in the beer. Add 1C of the cooked tomatoes, the tomato sauce, chili powder, salt, paprika, and cayenne pepper. Simmer covered until the chili is reduced to 3/4 gallon, about 3 hours. Stir occasionally. Skim any grease that appears at the top of the pan. Dissolve the masa harina in 3T water and stir into the chili. Simmer covered for 30 minutes.

Refrigerate overnight:
The flavors will blend as the chili sits.

Serves 12

EL TOVAR
Grand Canyon
Chef Esteban Colon

ROAST IOWA PORK TENDERLOIN WITH SAGE AND CIDER SAUCE

1-1/2T Flour
1/2t Sage
1t Salt
Freshly ground Pepper, to taste
2 lbs. Pork Tenderloin, trimmed and patted dry
2T hot Olive Oil
Sage and Cider Sauce, recipe follows

Coat:
Mix the flour, sage, salt, and pepper in a plastic bag. Add the pork and shake.

Brown 8 minutes:
On the stovetop, in a stove-to-oven casserole, brown the pork in oil. The casserole should be just large enough to hold the pork.

Bake 20 to 25 minutes:
Bake at 350 degrees.

Serve:
Spread Sage and Cider Sauce on a serving plate, and lay the pork on top.

Serves 5

SAGE AND CIDER SAUCE

3T Unsalted Butter
1/2C Onion, chopped
2 cloves Garlic, minced
1T Sage
1/2 Granny Smith Apple, peeled, cored and sliced
1/4C Calvados*
1/2C Cider
2C Chicken Stock
1T Cornstarch dissolved in water

*Calvados is a dry apple brandy.

Heat 20 minutes:
Melt the butter in a large, heavy saucepan. Add the onion, garlic, and sage. Saute 5 minutes. Add the apple, calvados, cider, and stock, and boil 15 minutes until the apples are cooked.

Puree.

Bring to a boil:
Return the pureed apple mixture to the saucepan, and bring to a boil again. If necessary, thicken slightly with cornstarch dissolved in water.

Strain:
Strain the sauce through a fine sieve.

THE
MANSION CLUB
Phoenix
Chef Peter Inauen

PORK CHOPS WITH APPLE CORNBREAD STUFFING

1t Salt
1/2t White Pepper
5 Pork Chops, 8 oz. each
Apple Cornbread Stuffing, recipe follows
1C Flour
6T Vegetable Oil
1C Beef Broth
1C Unsweetened Apple Juice
2 oz. Chopped Bacon (3 strips)
1 clove Garlic, chopped
1/2t Shallot, chopped
2T White Wine
Pinch of Cayenne Pepper
1t Brown Sugar
1T Arrowroot
4T Water

Prepare the stuffing:
Recipe below.

Coat and stuff:
With a boning knife, cut a pocket in the side of the pork chops opposite the bone. Pound to tenderize, being careful not to separate the meat from the bone. Rub the inside and outside of the chops with a mixture of salt and pepper. Fill the chops with equal amounts of stuffing. Fasten each opening with a toothpick, making sure the ends are exposed for easy removal. Flatten lightly to spread the stuffing. Dip the chops in flour.

Brown:
Brown both sides of the chops on the stove top in 6T vegetable oil.

Bake 50 minutes:

Place the chops, broth and apple juice in a baking dish or heavy pot. Cover tightly and bake at 375 degrees. When done, remove the toothpicks. Save 2 cups of the apple/beef broth for use in the sauce.

Heat 15 minutes:

Brown the bacon. Add the garlic and shallot, and saute lightly. Deglaze the pan with wine. In a bowl, mix the reserved apple/beef broth, cayenne, and brown sugar. Strain the mixture and add it to the pan. In another bowl, dissolve the arrowroot in cold water. Stir the mixture into the sauce until the sauce thickens.

Serves 5

APPLE CORNBREAD STUFFING

1/2C Flour, all purpose
1/2C Yellow Corn Meal
1t Baking Powder
1/2t Salt
1/2C Milk
1 Egg
1T Vegetable Shortening
1/2 medium Onion, diced
1 rib Celery, diced
1 Granny Smith Apple, diced
2T Butter
1C Apple Juice

Mix:

In a mixing bowl, combine the flour, corn meal, baking powder, and salt. Add the milk, egg, and shortening, and mix lightly. Don't overmix.

(continued on next page)

Bake 15 to 20 minutes:
Bake the mixture at 400 degrees in a greased pan until golden brown.
Cool.

Saute:
Heat the onion, celery, apple and butter until half cooked.

Mix:
Combine the saute with the baked flour mixture. Add apple juice
and mix lightly. More apple juice may be added if the stuffing
is too dry.

Rest 15 minutes.

**THE LANDMARK
RESTAURANT**
Mesa
Chef Eric Foust

BLACK BEAN
AND VENISON CHILI

This recipe is a Mexican Cookoff Gold Medal Winner.

    5 strips Bacon
    1/2 Onion, diced
    1C Black Beans
    2 cloves Garlic, minced
    1 bunch Cilantro, chopped
    4C Chicken Stock
    2 Anaheim Chilies, minced
    1-1/2 lbs. Venison
    Con Queso Blanco, recipe follows
    Red Pepper Coulis, recipe follows
    Tomato Salsa, recipe follows

    Garnish:
    Tortilla

Cook 4 hours:
Over medium-high heat, saute the bacon until crispy. Add the onion and saute 1 minute. Add the beans, garlic, cilantro, stock, and chilies. Bring to a boil, reduce heat, and simmer about 4 hours.

Prepare the sauces:
Recipes follow.

Deep fry:
Slice 1 tortilla, julienne. Deep fry.

Or deep fry a tortilla cup. Submerge a tortilla in hot oil. Hold a small metal sieve or other metal cup shaped object (open end up) on top of the tortilla. As the tortilla heats, it will rise and wrap around the metal cup. In a moment or two, the tortilla will turn golden brown. Remove it from the oil and the cup. It will maintain the cup shape.

(continued on next page)

Brown:
Quickly brown the venison in a hot saute pan.

Roast 8 to 10 minutes:
Bake the browned venison at 375 degrees. When done, cut into twelve 1/2 inch slices. Keep warm.

Serve:
Drizzle Con Queso Blanco in a circle around the edge of each plate. Sprinkle Red Pepper Coulis over the Con Queso Blanco. Place the Black Bean Chili in the center of the plate, and pile Tomato Salsa in the middle of the chili. Top with 2 slices of venison. Garnish with tortilla.

Serves 6

CON QUESO BLANCO

2T Ventana Chardonnay
2 cloves Garlic, minced
1/4 medium Onion, diced
1/2C Heavy Cream
1t Cumin
1/2t Salt
1T Cayenne Pepper
4 oz. Cream Cheese, lightly softened

Simmer several minutes:
Cook the chardonnay, garlic, and onion over medium heat until the liquid is reduced to half. Add the cream, cumin, salt, and cayenne. Simmer 4 minutes. Whisk in the cream cheese. Strain.

RED PEPPER COULIS

2 Sweet Red Peppers, diced
2 cloves Garlic, minced
1/4C Chicken Stock
Salt and Pepper, to taste

Simmer 15 minutes, then puree.

TOMATO SALSA

2 large, ripe Tomatoes, seeded and diced
1/4 Onion, diced
2 cloves Garlic, minced
1 Anaheim Chili, roasted and diced*
1/2 Sweet Yellow Pepper, roasted and diced
1/2 Sweet Red Pepper, roasted and diced
1/2 bunch Cilantro, chopped
Salt and Pepper, to taste

*The Appendix lists several methods for roasting
chilies. Mr. Fields recommends roasting over an
open flame.

Mix all the ingredients and serve at room temperature.

LOEWS VENTANA
CANYON RESORT
VENTANA ROOM
Tucson
Chef Tim Fields

POULTRY

Kabali Palaw

Pollo Papagallo

Farfalle Pasta Alvolo

Chicken Mole

Sizzling Chicken Fajitas

Enchilada Nuda

Tequila-Lime Chicken Strips
with Pineapple-Tomatillo Salsa

Arroz con Pollo

Cashew Nut Chicken

Grilled Range Chicken Scallopini
with Hunan Peanut Sauce

Pad Gra Prao Gai

Oven Fried Sesame-Cilantro
Chicken

Hawaiian Chicken Breast

Chicken Breast Bombay

Sherried Leek, Squash, and
Mushroom Stew

Chicken Bon Fem

Medallions of Chicken Breasts
in Green Peppercorn Sauce

Macadamia Chicken with
Dijon Pesto Cream

Herb Roasted Chicken with
Tomato Coulis

Chicken Neptune

Mogollon Duck Courvoisier

Smoked Muscovy Duck with
Mesquite Grilled Vegetable
Galantine "Fajita Style"

Duck and Papaya Quesadilla

Sliced Duck Breast with
Burgundy Sauce and
Kiwi Garnish

KABALI PALAW
Chicken Pilaf

A highly acclaimed traditional Afghani dish.

> 1 Onion
> 1/4C Oil
> 1t Cumin
> 1/2t Black Cardamom, ground*
> 1/2t Black Pepper
> 2t Salt
> Dash of Cinnamon
> 3C Water
> 1 Chicken, whole or in pieces
> 1/2C Raisins
> 3 Carrots, 2 to 3 inch julienne
> 1t regular ground Cardamom
> Dash of Sugar
> 3C Basmati Rice
> Slivered Almonds, optional

*Regular cardamom may be used if dark is not available.

Simmer the chicken and sauce 25 minutes:
Puree the onion and oil. If you do not have a blender, you can use minced onions. Saute the puree until it turns dark brown. Mix the cumin, black cardamom, pepper, salt, and cinnamon in a small bowl. Add the water and 1/3 of the spice mixture to the saute pan. Set the remaining spices aside. Add the chicken and simmer, covered, for about 20 minutes, until the chicken is 3/4 done.

Remove the chicken from the skillet, saving the sauce. Add the reserved spices to the sauce. The total sauce volume should be approximately 1-3/4C. If not, add water.

Saute the carrots and raisins 10 minutes:
Saute the raisins with 1 drop of oil and 1 drop of water over low heat. Stir the raisins occasionally while cooking. When the raisins are barely soft, remove them from the pan. Add the carrots, regular cardamom, and sugar to the raisin pan. Saute 5 minutes.

Boil the rice 5 minutes:
Place the rice in a pot with enough water to cover the rice by 3 to 4 inches. Boil 4 to 5 minutes with the lid off. Watch the rice to make sure it cooks evenly. To test for doneness, bite a piece. The rice is done when you hear a little, dry, cracking sound. Drain the water with a strainer.

Bake 30 minutes:
Place the rice in a 2 quart roasting pan. Cover the rice with sauce. Bury the chicken in the rice, and bury the raisins and carrots in one corner. For extra color and texture, slivered almonds may be added to the carrots and raisins. Cover and bake at 375 degrees.

Serve:
Place the chicken on a large platter and smother it with rice. Sprinkle the carrots and raisins on top. This dish is traditionally eaten with Bohn Jon Bouranee (see Side Dishes).

Serves 4 to 6

CHOPANDAZ
AFGHANI RESTAURANT
Tempe
Chef Shuja Ahmad

POLLO PAPPAGALLO

1/4C Cornstarch
4 Eggs
1C Seasoned Bread Crumbs
4 Chicken Breasts, boneless
8 slices Mozzarella Cheese
Pepper Sauce, recipe follows

Coat:
Dip the chicken in a mixture of cornstarch and eggs, then in the breadcrumbs.

Deep fry and broil:
Deep fry the breaded chicken until golden. When done, drain well, and place the chicken in oven proof dishes. Lay the cheese on top of the chicken and broil until the cheese melts.

Serve:
Spoon Pepper Sauce over the chicken.

Serves 4

PEPPER SAUCE

2T Vegetable Oil
2 1/2C Onion, chopped
2 cloves Garlic, minced
Pinch of Flour, to thicken
1/2C sweet Cherry Peppers, chopped
1/2C sweet Red Bell Peppers, chopped
1C White Mushrooms, sliced
1/4C Chicken Broth
1/8C Sherry Wine
Salt and Pepper, to taste

Heat several minutes:
Saute the onion and garlic until golden. Add the flour and stir. Add the remaining ingredients and simmer for a few minutes.

HASSAYAMPA INN
Prescott
Chef Linda Rose

'ALLE PASTA ALVOLO
w Tie Pasta

Tie Pasta
preferably extra virgin
2 cloves Garlic, minced
2 Chicken Breasts (boneless, skinless, sliced
into thin slivers)
1/4 lb. Mushrooms, your favorite kind
2T Pine Nuts
4 Artichoke Hearts, cut into wedges
Salt and Pepper to taste
1T Butter
1/4C White Wine
1/2C Chicken Broth

Boil:
Boil the pasta in lightly salted water until al dente. Rinse and drain.

Grill or saute several minutes:
Cook the chicken over a grill or skillet until done.

Saute and simmer 10 to 15 minutes:
Saute the garlic in oil over medium heat. Cook until golden.
Remove the garlic. Add the chicken, mushrooms, pine nuts,
artichoke hearts, salt, and pepper. Cook for a few minutes. Add the
butter, wine, and broth. Reduce 5 to 10 minutes. Add the cooked
pasta and heat for a moment until hot.

Serves 4

RAFFAELE'S
Phoenix
Chef Raffaele Contacessi

139

CHICKEN MOLE

12 Chicken Breast halves, skinless and boneless
2C Tomato Sauce (15 oz. can)
3/4C Green Bell Pepper, diced
1/4C Cocoa
1/2C Almonds, slivered
3/4C Onion, chopped
3 cloves Garlic
1/4C Brown Sugar
2T Corn Syrup
2t Sesame Seeds
1/2t Cinammon
1 Bay Leaf, crumbled
2t Salt
1/4t Pepper
2t Chile Powder
1/8t Cloves, ground
2T Canola Oil
Garnish:
Lime slices
Sesame Seeds

Brown and simmer 35 to 40 minutes:
Brown the chicken in oil. Add just enough water to cover the chicken, and simmer 30 minutes. When done, keep the chicken in the pan, and remove the broth. Save 1 cup of broth. You will add it to the sauce, below.

Blend:
Blend the remaining ingredients in a food processor. Add the reserved broth and blend.

Simmer 30 minutes:
Pour the blended mixture into the chicken pan and simmer 30 more minutes.

Serve:
Serve garnished with lime slices and sesame seeds.

Serves 6

THE TACK ROOM
Tucson
The Kane and Vactor Family

140

SIZZLING CHICKEN FAJITAS

4T Olive Oil
1 Green Bell Pepper, cut in strips
1 Onion, cut in strips
1 lb. Chicken Breasts, cut in strips
2T Fajita Seasoning
Juice of 1/2 Lime
6 to 8 Flour Tortillas
Lettuce
Tomato, diced
Cheddar Cheese
Sour Cream
Guacamole

Saute 8 minutes:
To make this dish really sizzle, saute in a cast iron skillet. Saute the pepper, onion, and chicken in oil over medium heat for 5 minutes. Cook until the chicken is just done. Add the fajita seasoning and lime juice, and heat through for 3 minutes.

Serve:
Serve with the tortillas, lettuce, tomato, cheese, sour cream, and guacamole. Place the fillings on a side dish, and let your guests roll their own fajitas.

Serves 2

MICHAEL'S
FINE DINING
Page
Chef Michael J. Decker

ENCHILADA NUDA
Nude Enchilada

This enchilada is served without a tortilla wrapping.

> 4 pieces Gouda Cheese, 7 oz. each, room
>   temperature, hollowed
> 8 oz. Chicken Breast, sliced thin
> 1/2 Green Pepper, sliced thin
> 1T Red Onion, diced
> Pinch of Chile Powder
> Salt and Pepper to taste

Saute few minutes:
Saute the chicken, with pepper, onion, chile powder, salt and pepper until the chicken is just done.

Broil few minutes:
Place the chicken mixture in the hollowed cheese. Glaze under a broiler until the cheese turns a light, golden brown.

Serve:
Spread Nuda Sauce on a serving plate, and lay the chicken and cheese on top.

Serves 4

NUDA SAUCE

2 Tomatoes, diced
1 Red Onion, diced
1 clove Garlic, diced
1 Jalapeño, diced
1 large green Anaheim Chile
1t Cumin
1/4t Oregano
1/2t Chile Powder
1C Tomato Juice

Saute and boil 8 to 10 minutes:
Saute the tomatoes, onion, garlic, jalapeño, and chile over low heat.
Heat 3 to 4 minutes, until the vegetables are slightly cooked. Add the
cumin, oregano, chile powder, and tomato juice, and bring to a boil.
Once the mixture is boiling, skim the froth and mix well.

**INN AT
McCORMICK RANCH**
PIÑON GRILL
Scottsdale
Chef Farn Boggie

TEQUILA-LIME CHICKEN STRIPS WITH PINEAPPLE-TOMATILLO SALSA

1/2C Lime Juice
1/3C Golden Tequila
1/4C Olive Oil
2T Cointreau
2 cloves Garlic, minced
4 Chicken Breasts, 6 oz. each, boneless and
   skinless, cut into strips.
1/4t Salt
1/8t freshly ground Pepper
Pineapple-Tomatillo Salsa, recipe follows

Marinate 2 hours or overnight:
In a large bowl, combine the lime juice, tequila, olive oil, Cointreau, and garlic. Thread the chicken breasts onto bamboo skewers. Place the skewers in the marinade, and turn to coat completely. Marinate for 2 hours at room temperature, or overnight in the refrigerator, returning the chicken to room temperature before cooking.

Bake 10 to 12 minutes:
Season the marinated chicken with salt and pepper. Place the chicken skewers on a baking sheet. Bake at 400 degrees on your oven's upper rack.

Serve:
Serve with Pineapple-Tomatillo Salsa.

Serves 4

PINEAPPLE-TOMATILLO SALSA

1-1/2C Pineapple, finely chopped
5 small fresh Tomatillos, finely chopped
1/2 Jalepeño Pepper or 1 Serrano Chile, seeded
  and minced
2T to 1C fresh Lime Juice, to taste
1/4t Salt
1-1/4C Pineapple, finely diced
1/4C fresh Coriander, minced

Puree:
Puree the 1-1/2C pineapple, tomatillos, jalapeño, lime juice and salt
until smooth. Pour the puree into a bowl and stir in 1-1/4C
pineapple and coriander. If desired, add more salt and up to 1C lime
juice, to taste.

Let sit 1 hour:
Cover and let sit at room temperature.

Serves 4 to 6

ENCHANTMENT
RESORT
Sedona
Chef Gerald Peters

ARROZ CON POLLO
Rice with Chicken

3 lbs. Chicken, cut into 8 pieces
2t Salt
1t Pepper
4T Olive Oil
1 large Green Bell Pepper, finely chopped
1 large Red Bell Pepper, finely chopped
1 large Yellow Onion, finely chopped
4 large Garlic Cloves, finely chopped
2C Long Grain Rice, uncooked
2t Salt
2t Pepper
2t Oregano, dried
2 Bay Leaves
1/4t Saffron
1t Ground Cumin
1/2 lb. Spanish Chorizo, semidry*
1/2C White Wine
1C Chicken Broth
1C Water

Garnish:
White Asparagus Spears
Canned Peas
Pimento Strips

*Mexican chorizo is not a good substitute for this
recipe. If Spanish is not available, you can
prepare the dish without chorizo.

Saute & simmer 35 minutes:
Season the chicken with salt and pepper. Saute with 2T olive oil over medium heat until lightly browned. Set aside.

In a Dutch oven or heavy covered pot, lightly saute the peppers, onion, and garlic in 2T oil. If you are using the same skillet the chicken was fried in, pour off the used oil and add 2T fresh oil.

Add the rice, 2t salt, 2t pepper, oregano, bay leaves, saffron and cumin. Stir until coated. Add the sauteed chicken, chorizo, wine, broth and water. Bring to a boil, reduce heat, stir well, and cover. Simmer for 20 minutes, until the rice is tender. If after 20 minutes all the liquid has not been absorbed, remove from heat and let sit, covered, for 5 minutes.

Serve:
Spoon the chicken and rice onto a serving dish. Garnish with white asparagus spears, canned peas, and pimento strips, all at room temperature.

Serves 4

HAVANA CAFE
Phoenix
The Hernandez Family

CASHEW NUT CHICKEN

Rice or Noodles to yield 2C
1/8C Oil
2C Chicken Breasts, sliced
1C Onion, sliced
1/2C Mushrooms, sliced
3C Chinese Cabbage, sliced
1/2C Bamboo Shoots, sliced
1C Snow Peas, whole or cut
1C Celery, thinly sliced
1/2C Water Chestnuts, sliced
1-1/2t Salt
1t Sugar
1T Soy Sauce
2C Chicken Broth
4T Cornstarch
3t Red or White Wine
1C Cashews

Boil:
Prepare your favorite rice or noodles.

Cook in a wok:
Heat a wok over high heat. Add the oil and swirl. Add the chicken and onion and stir until the chicken turns white. Add the mushrooms, cabbage, bamboo shoots, snow peas, celery, water chestnuts, salt, sugar, soy sauce, and chicken broth. Cover and simmer for a few minutes. Remove any excess liquid. The liquid should reach half the height of the vegetables. Dissolve the cornstarch and wine in a bowl. Add the mixture directly into the

hot broth. Stir until the gravy thickens. If the mixture is not stirred thoroughly, the vegetables will stick together. The gravy is done when it becomes a clear glaze.

Turn off the heat. Add the cashews and stir.

Serve:
Serve the chicken over rice or noodles.

Serves 4

HOUSE OF CHAN
Kingman
Chef Tommy Chan

GRILLED RANGE CHICKEN SCALLOPINI WITH HUNAN PEANUT SAUCE

10 Chicken Breast halves, boned, skins removed
   and pounded thin
1/4C Flour
2T Peanut Oil
Hunan Peanut Sauce, recipe follows

Coat:
Coat the chicken with flour.

Saute 15 minutes:
Brown the chicken in oil over medium heat. Cook 7 to 8 minutes on
each side, until it is fully cooked.

Serve:
Strain Hunan Peanut Sauce through a sieve over the chicken.

Serves 5

HUNAN PEANUT SAUCE

1/4C Butter, unsalted
4 Green Onions, sliced
3 cloves Garlic, minced
1t Ginger, grated
1/2t Sichuan Peppercorns, ground
2 Pickled Red Chile Peppers, chopped
1T Sherry
2T Soy Sauce
1C Chicken Stock
1C Peanut Butter, creamy style

Heat 20 minutes:
Heat the butter in a large heavy skillet over low heat. Add the green
onions, garlic, ginger, peppercorns, and peppers. Saute for 3 minutes.
Add sherry and soy sauce. Simmer 2 minutes. Add chicken stock,
and boil for 8 minutes. Add the peanut butter, and just bring to a
boil, stirring constantly.

THE MANSION CLUB
Phoenix
Chef Peter Inauen

PAD GRA PRAO GAI
Minted Stir Fry

1T Oil
1C Chicken, sliced
1/2t Garlic, chopped
1/4-1/2t Chile Powder
1-1/2t Fish Sauce
1-1/2t thin Soy Sauce
2 to 3T Chicken Broth
1/2t fresh Thai Chile (Prig Kinu) or
  sliced Jalapeño chile
8 to 10 leaves fresh Thai Sweet Basil or Mint

Saute and simmer 15 minutes:
Heat the oil over high heat until it becomes hot. Add the chicken,
garlic, chile powder, fish sauce, and soy sauce. Cook 3 minutes,
stirring. Add the chicken broth and cook 7 to 10 minutes, until the
chicken is done. Add the Thai chile and basil or mint and cook for a
few minutes.

Serves 2 to 4

**PINK PEPPER
THAI CUISINE**
Scottsdale, Mesa, Phoenix
Chef Tony Tavee

OVEN FRIED SESAME-CILANTRO CHICKEN

4T Soy Sauce
4T Flour, all purpose
3T Sesame Seeds
3T fresh Cilantro or Italian Parsley, chopped
1/2t Salt
12 Chicken Breasts, boneless and skinless
4T Butter or Margarine, melted

Coat:
Place the soy sauce in a shallow dish. Mix the flour, sesame seeds, cilantro, and salt on waxed paper. Coat the chicken with soy sauce. Then dip the flesh side in the flour mixture. Drizzle butter over the chicken.

Bake 50 minutes:
Bake the chicken at 400 degrees until it is fork tender. Baste once during the cooking period with drippings from the pan. Keep covered until the last few minutes. Then remove the cover to allow browning.

Serves 6

THE TACK ROOM
Tucson
The Kane and Vactor Family

HAWAIIAN CHICKEN BREAST

1 serving of your favorite noodles
Pinch of Garlic, granulated
Pinch of Seasoned Salt
Dab of Butter, melted
Parmesan Cheese, grated, to taste
1 Chicken Breast, boneless and skinless
Pinch of Granulated Garlic
Pinch of Seasoned Salt
Pinch of Pepper
2 thin slices Canadian Bacon
2 thin slices Fresh Pineapple
1 slice Big-Eye Swiss Cheese or Gruyere

Boil:
Boil the noodles. When done, drain, and season with garlic, salt, butter, and Parmesan cheese.

Saute and broil:
Season the chicken with garlic, salt, and pepper, to taste. Saute 4 minutes per side, until the chicken is just done. Remove it from the pan. Heat the bacon and pineapple in the chicken pan for 1 minute on each side. Top the chicken with the bacon, pineapple, and cheese. Broil, bake, or fry the chicken(covered), just long enough to melt the cheese.

Serve:
Serve the chicken with warm seasoned noodles.

Serves 1

RANCHO DE LOS CABALLEROS
Wickenburg
Chef Daniel Martin

154

CHICKEN BREAST BOMBAY

Zest of 2 Lemons
Juice of 1/2 Lemon
1C Olive Oil
1/2C Bombay Gin
1/2 Red Onion, chopped
1/2t Juniper Berries, crushed
1 Carrot, chopped
1 Bay Leaf
2 dashes of Tabasco Sauce
1t Salt
12 Chicken Breast halves, boneless and skinless

Marinate overnight:
In a bowl, mix the grated lemon skins, lemon juice, olive oil, gin, onion, berries, carrot, bay leaf, Tabasco sauce, and salt. Add the chicken and refrigerate overnight. Turn several times.

Grill or broil 10 to 14 minutes:
Grill the chicken over a medium heat barbecue or broiler, 5 to 7 minutes each side.

Serves 6

SOLARIUM
RESTAURANT
Tucson
Chef Jonathan Landeen

SHERRIED LEEK, SQUASH, AND MUSHROOM STEW

Olive Oil, to coat pan
3C Mushrooms, sliced
3C Leeks, julienne
1-1/2C Zucchini Squash, sliced
1-1/2C Yellow Squash, julienne
4T Garlic, chopped
3/4C Sherry
1/2C Chicken Stock
3C Tomatoes, chopped
2C Scallions, diagonally cut
Salt and Pepper, to taste

Saute and simmer several minutes:
Heat olive oil in a large saute pan, over high heat. Saute the mushrooms, leeks, zucchini, yellow squash, and garlic. Add the garlic last. Saute until the vegetables are almost done. Add the sherry and ignite to burn off the alcohol. Add the chicken stock and simmer 3 minutes. Add the tomatoes, scallions, salt, and pepper. Simmer 1 minute.

Serves 6

JANOS
Tucson
Chef Janos Wilder

CHICKEN BON FEM

2C Rice
4 Chicken Breasts, 8 oz. each
1/2C Flour
4 oz. clarified Butter
2 cloves Garlic, chopped finely
1 Cucumber, chopped
2 Tomatoes, chopped
1/2t Parsley, chopped
1t Black Pepper
2C Chablis Wine

Steam:
Steam the rice.

Coat:
Dust the chicken with flour.

Saute and simmer 35 minutes:
Saute the chicken in butter over medium heat. When browned on one side, turn, and add the garlic. Add the cucumber, tomatoes, parsley, and black pepper. Cook 25 minutes, until the chicken is tender. Add the wine and simmer covered, for 2 minutes.

Serve:
Serve over a bed of rice.

Serves 4

BIG MAN'S CATERING
Kingman
Chef Watkin Sells

MEDALLIONS OF CHICKEN BREASTS IN GREEN PEPPERCORN SAUCE

12 Chicken Breasts, skinless and boneless
6T Unsalted Butter
4 Shallots, minced
2 large Carrots, finely chopped
3/4 lb. Mushrooms, diced fine (2C whole mushrooms)
3/8t Salt
3/8t Black Pepper, freshly ground
24 to 30 large Spinach leaves, (1 head)
20 slices Prosciutto Ham, sliced thin
Raw egg wash
Egg, beaten
Flour
6C Bread Crumbs, fresh toasted
1T Oregano, dried
1T Basil, dried
1T Thyme, dried
Green Peppercorn Sauce, recipe follows

Preparation:
Pound the chicken until it is evenly thin and square. To reduce the chance of tearing the chicken, pound it inside 2 closable plastic bags.

Saute the butter and shallots until the shallots become translucent. Add the carrots and mushrooms and saute until most liquid is gone. Season with salt and pepper.

Dip the spinach in boiling water until the leaves just turn limp and bright green. Keep the leaves as whole as possible.

Form rolls:

Lay the smooth side of the chicken down, and spread a thin layer (2T) sauteed mixture on each piece. Top each piece with spinach and ham. Roll the chicken, starting at the large side. To keep the chicken rolled, paint the surface with raw egg, beaten. Dip the painted rolls in flour, then in more beaten egg, then in a mixture of bread crumbs, oregano, basil, and thyme.

Brown, then bake 15 minutes:

Saute the rolls in olive oil until brown. Bake 15 minutes at 400 degrees.

Serve:

Spread Green Peppercorn Sauce on a serving platter. Carve the chicken rolls into 1/2 inch thick slices. Arrange them on the sauce, overlapping.

Serves 12

GREEN PEPPERCORN SAUCE

2 Shallots, chopped fine
6 oz. can Green Peppercorns, drained (save juice)
1/4C Burgundy Wine
1 qt. Sauce Demiglaze

Heat 5 to 10 minutes:

Saute the shallots in butter. Add the drained peppercorns and heat until hot. Deglaze with wine. Add the demiglaze and peppercorn juice, and heat until hot.

THE TACK ROOM
Tucson
The Kane and Vactor Family

MACADAMIA CHICKEN WITH DIJON PESTO CREAM

    4 whole Chicken Breasts, skinned,
      pounded lightly
    7 Eggs, beaten
    1-1/2C Macadamia Nuts, ground
    Clarified Butter, to coat pan
    Dijon Pesto Cream Sauce, recipe follows

    Garnish:
    Basil
    Red Bell Pepper, julienne

Coat:
Dip the chicken in the beaten eggs, then roll in the nuts.

Brown, then bake 8 to 10 minutes:
Saute the chicken in butter until evenly browned on both sides.
Bake at 350 degrees.

Serve:
Cover the bottom of a plate with Dijon Pesto Cream Sauce and lay
the chicken on top. Garnish with fresh basil and red bell pepper,
julienne.

Serves 4

BASIL PESTO

    1/2C Pine Nuts
    3C Basil Leaves, freshly picked
    2t Garlic, finely minced
    1/4C good Olive Oil

Puree:
Blend the basil and garlic in a food processor. Add the oil slowly, and
puree on high speed until a paste forms.

Yields 3 Cups

DIJON PESTO CREAM SAUCE

Clarified Butter, to coat pan
1t Garlic, finely minced
1t Shallot, finely minced
1 qt. Heavy Cream
4T Dijon Mustard
3T Basil Pesto, recipe above
Salt and Pepper to taste

Saute for a few minutes:
Saute the garlic and shallot in a buttered skillet over medium heat.
Add the cream and mustard, and reduce by half.

Whisk in:
Remove from heat and whisk in the pesto, salt, and pepper.

Yields 1 Quart

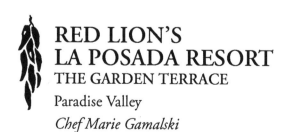

RED LION'S
LA POSADA RESORT
THE GARDEN TERRACE
Paradise Valley
Chef Marie Gamalski

HERB ROASTED CHICKEN WITH TOMATO COULIS

Featuring a fabulous blend of herbs and spices, this dish is low in cholesterol, sodium, and calories.

4 Chicken Breasts, 8 oz. each,
  skinless and boneless
1T fresh Basil, chopped
1T fresh Thyme, chopped
1T fresh Rosemary, chopped
1T fresh Oregano, chopped
1T Sun-dried Tomatoes, chopped
1t ground Black Pepper
1t crushed Red Chilies
1/2C Olive Oil
2 cloves Garlic, minced
1/2C White Wine
Tomato Coulis, recipe follows

Marinate 4 hours:
Place the chicken in a mixture of all the ingredients except the wine and Tomato Coulis. Marinate for at least 4 hours.

Saute and simmer 10 minutes:
Place the marinated chicken breasts directly in a large heated saute pan over medium heat. Saute 3-1/2 minutes per side, turning twice while cooking. Add the wine and simmer for 3 minutes.

Serve:
Serve with Tomato Coulis.

Serves 4

TOMATO COULIS

1 clove Garlic, minced
4 whole Tomatoes, peeled and deseeded
1 Yellow Onion, chopped
1C Chicken Stock

Saute and simmer 18 minutes:
Saute the garlic. Add the tomatoes, onion, and chicken
stock, and simmer 15 minutes.

Puree:
Puree in a blender and adjust seasoning to taste.

THE
ARIZONA CLUB
Scottsdale
Chef Scott Tompkins

CHICKEN NEPTUNE

A treat for the chicken-seafood lover.

     4 oz. Crabmeat
     2 oz. Bay Shrimp
     1 Shallot, chopped
     2 Scallions, chopped
     1t Parsley, chopped
     Pinch of Garlic
     1T Butter, melted
     4 Chicken Breasts, 8 oz. each, skinless
     2 Eggs
     1T Milk
     Mornay Sauce, recipe follows

Stuff:
Cut a pocket in the chicken on the side opposite the keel bone.
Stuff with a mixture of crabmeat, shrimp, shallot, scallions, parsley, garlic, and butter.

Coat:
In a bowl, beat the eggs and milk. Coat the breasts with flour, then egg mixture, and flour again.

Brown, then bake 20 minutes:
Brown the chicken on both sides. Then bake in a 350 degree oven for 20 minutes.

Serve:
Top with Mornay Sauce and serve.

Serves 4

MORNAY SAUCE

2C Chicken Stock
2C Heavy Cream
1C Swiss Cheese, grated
Pinch of granulated Garlic
Pinch of White Pepper
Pinch of Cayenne Pepper
Roux, as needed
1/2C grated Parmesan Cheese
1C Chardonnay Wine

Heat several minutes:
In a double boiler, heat the chicken stock, cream, swiss cheese, garlic, white pepper, and cayenne pepper. Add the ingredients in the order listed, mixing after each addition. Cook until the mixture becomes creamy. Add roux, as needed, to make the sauce very thick. Add the Parmesan cheese and stir until blended. Add the wine and blend.

Serves 4

BIG MAN'S CATERING
Kingman
Chef Watkin Sells

MOGOLLON DUCK COURVOISIER

The breast of the Muscovy Duck is very meaty and flavorful. We use ducks from Grimaud Farms in Linden, California.

3 Muscovy Duck Breasts, double, boneless*
1 qt. Mogollon Marinade, recipe follows
2C Courvoisier Sauce, recipe follows
Garnish:
1/2C Candied Walnuts
Fresh Baby Vegetables

*You may use other duck breasts, but you will need to vary the quantity and cooking times.

Marinate 24 hours:
Marinate the duck in Mogollon Marinade.

Roast 45 minutes:
Place the breasts on a rack, over a roasting pan, in the oven. Roast at 200 degrees. Roasting slowly reduces the fattiness of the final dish. Let cool when done.

Sear 8 minutes:
In a hot pan on the stove top, without oil, sear the duck, skin side down, for 7 minutes. Turn over and sear 1 minute. The meat may darken slightly. Searing is done to seal in the juices.

Roast 5 minutes:
Place the breasts in a pie tin. Bake at 400 degrees until the meat is medium rare, pink and rosy all the way through. Let rest 5 minutes before carving.

Serve:
Using a sharp, thin knife, remove the skin. Carve the duck into thin slices on a diagonal, against the grain. Fan the slices out on a warm plate. Cover with Courvoisier Sauce and garnish with 1/2C candied walnuts and fresh baby vegetables.

Serves 6

MOGOLLON MARINADE

2C Soy Sauce
2T Garlic, fresh crushed
2T Ginger Root, fresh chopped
1C Scotch
1C Water
1C Brown Sugar
1/2C Lime Juice

Mix well.

Yields 1 quart

COURVOISIER SAUCE

1-1/2t Garlic, minced
1-1/2t Shallots, minced
1-1/2t fresh Ginger, minced
1/4C Courvoisier
1/4C Orange Curacao or Triple Sec
1/2C Orange Juice
1/8C Brown Sugar
1-1/2C Demi-Glaze
2T Cornstarch
Salt and Pepper to taste

Saute and simmer:
Saute the garlic, shallots, and ginger until the shallots become translucent. Add the Courvoisier and Orange Curacao and reduce by half. Add the orange juice and brown sugar and bring to a boil. Add demiglaze and simmer for 10 minutes. Thicken with cornstarch, and season with salt and pepper.

Yields 2 Cups

WESTCOURT IN THE BUTTES
TOP OF THE ROCK
Tempe
Chef Franklin Biggs

SMOKED MUSCOVY DUCK WITH MESQUITE GRILLED VEGETABLE GALANTINE "FAJITA STYLE"

4 Spanish Onions, sliced
2C Consomme
2T Sugar
Salt and Pepper, to taste
4 fresh Artichoke Bottoms

2C Consomme
1T Olive Oil
3T Lemon Juice
1T Juniper Berries
1/2 bunch fresh Thyme, or 1t dried

4 Yellow Squash, sliced
4 Zucchini, sliced
2 Eggplant, sliced
5 Tomatoes, peeled, seeded, and quartered
Olive Oil
2 Sweet Yellow Peppers
2 Green Bell Peppers

1-1/2 to 2 Smoked Duck Breasts, sliced paper thin*
1/2 bunch Basil, finely chopped or whole leaf
Sheet gelatin*
Salt and Pepper, to taste

*Smoked duck is sold in Chinese markets. 3-inch gelatin
sheets can be purchased in most grocery stores.

Cook the vegetables:
Roast and peel the peppers. The appendix describes ways to do so.
Use the broiler method until the skins turn black.

Saute the onions, consomme, sugar, salt and pepper over medium
heat 10 to 15 minutes. Cook until most of the liquid has evaporated,

the remaining liquid is thick, and the onions appear glazed.

Place the artichoke crowns, consomme, olive oil, lemon juice, juniper berries, and thyme in another pan. Bring to a boil, reduce the heat, and simmer 10 to 15 minutes, or until the artichokes are soft. When done, drain and slice the artichoke bottoms.

Cook the squash, zucchini, and eggplant on a mesquite grill or nonstick pan. Heat, without oil, until the vegetables are almost done.

Saute the tomatoes in olive oil over medium heat for a few seconds on each side.

When all vegetables are prepared and laid out on sheet pans, lightly sprinkle with salt and pepper.

Melt the gelatin:
Soak the gelatin leaves in cold water until they become soft. Squeeze to remove the water. Turn a burner to low; when the burner warms, turn it off. Immediately place the gelatin leaves in the pan and watch them melt (seconds). Remove from heat.

Fill the terrine:
Line a terrine with the eggplant slices. Arrange alternate horizontal layers of vegetables, basil, and duck in the terrine. Brush each layer with a little gelatin as you go along. Place a weight on top of the terrine.

Refrigerate 6 to 8 hours:
Handle the terrine very gently as you place it in the refrigerator. After chilling, the gelatin will have hardened, and will hold the duck and vegetables more firmly.

Serve:
Slice into 1-inch
thick slices.

Serves 4

ARIZONA
BILTMORE RESORT
ORANGERIE
Phoenix
Chef Peter Hoefler

DUCK AND PAPAYA QUESADILLA

Gold Medal winner at the annual Southwest Mexican Cookoff.

> 2 Duck Breasts
> Salt and Pepper, to taste
> 1/2 White Onion, julienne
> 1 Red Sweet Pepper, julienne
> 1 Green Bell Pepper, julienne
> 1 Yellow Sweet Pepper, julienne
> 2T Ancho Puree
> 1/2C Demi Glaze
> 2 Flour or Blue Corn Tortillas
> 1 Papaya, cut into strips
> Tomato Salsa, recipe follows

Preparation, 10 to 15 minutes:
Season the duck with salt and pepper. Roast in a 400 degree oven for 7 to 10 minutes until the duck is medium rare.

In another pan, saute the onion and peppers over high heat for 1-1/2 to 3 minutes. Season to taste and set aside.

In a small bowl, mix the ancho puree and demiglaze.
Gently warm the tortillas in the oven, or on an open burner.

Fill the tortillas:
Lay the pepper mixture on half of each tortilla. Slice the duck breast into strips and place the strips on the pepper mixture. Lay the papaya between the strips of duck. Drizzle the ancho-demi puree on top. Fold the tortilla over and garnish with Tomato Salsa.

Serves 2

TOMATO SALSA

6 Roma Tomatoes
1/4 Onion, chopped
24 sprigs Cilantro, chopped
Juice from 1 Lime
1/4 Jalapeño Pepper, chopped
1/2t Ancho Chile Puree
Salt and Pepper, to taste

Combine.

**LOEWS VENTANA
CANYON RESORT**
VENTANA ROOM
Tucson
Chef Brian Light

SLICED DUCK BREAST WITH BURGUNDY SAUCE AND KIWI GARNISH

8 oz. Duck Breast
4T Butter
2 medium Shallots, chopped
1T Brandy
4T Red Wine
1/2C Brown Sauce or Red Wine
2T Butter

Garnish:
Kiwi
Squash
Zucchini
Red Potato

Saute and simmer:
Saute the duck until medium rare. Remove the duck, and fan the breast on a holding plate.

Add 4T butter, shallots, brandy and wine to the duck pan and saute over medium heat 10 minutes. Add the brown sauce or red wine and reduce by half. Strain the sauce through a fine sieve. Add 2T butter and heat until blended.

Serve:
Sauce the plate, and lay the fanned duck breast on the sauce. Set 3 slices of kiwi on top, and garnish with squash, zucchini, and red potato.

Yields 2 Entrees
or 3 Appetizers

LOEWS VENTANA CANYON RESORT
VENTANA ROOM
Tucson
Chef Takashi Shiramizu

SEAFOOD

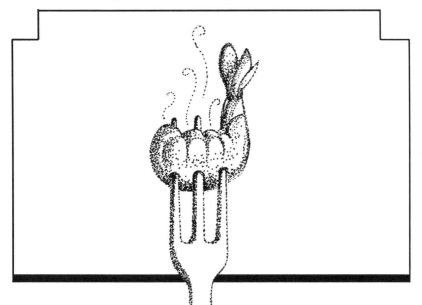

Tarragon Seared Ono with Pineapple and Passion Fruit Glaze

Seared Ahi Tuna with Shiitake Mushrooms and Sauce Naturelle

Catfish New Orleans

Fried Catfish with Creole Mustard Sauce

Red Snapper in Beer Dough

Linguine with Smoked Salmon

Grilled Salmon with Tomato Basil Butter Sauce

Braised Salmon with Mint and Sorrel Tomato Coulis

Oven Poached Dorado with Shrimp Mousse

Tuna Scallion Fiesta

Shrimp Al'Indiane

Shrimp Puerto Penasco

Shrimp Marie

Maricopa County Scampi

Scampi Vera Cruz

Scampi Napolitana

Scampi El Conquistador

Spaghettini Portofino

Gulf of Siam

Pasta Shellfish

Tabbuleh of Sea Scallops with Cucumbers and Tomatoes in Lime Vinaigrette

Fettucine with Scallops and Shiitake Mushrooms

Seafood Linguine

Angel Hair Pasta, Fresh Arizona Escargot in a Garlic Cream Sauce

Lobster Savannah

Blue Corn Crusted Chile Relleno with Lobster and Orange Chipotle Cream Sauce

TARRAGON SEARED ONO WITH PINEAPPLE AND PASSION FRUIT GLAZE

Also known as king mackerel, ono is one of Hawaii's most flavorful fish. Firm, white, meaty, and moist, ono in Hawaiian means "The best, number one!"

Ono:
2-1/4 lbs. Ono, cut into 12 slices, 1/2 inch thick
1 qt. Orange Juice
1C Flour
1t Salt
2T dried Tarragon Leaves
1/2t Garlic Powder
Pinch of White Pepper
Clarified Butter, to coat pan

Glaze:
2T Shallots, chopped
1T Pickled Ginger, chopped
1/2C Pineapple, finely diced
1 qt. Orange Juice
1C Passion Fruit Puree or Juice
1/2C White Wine
1/4C Cream
1 lb. Unsalted Butter, in pieces, cold
Salt and pepper to taste

Garnish:
Tropical Fruit such as banana, kiwi, pineapple, and papaya

Marinate 20 minutes and coat:
Marinate the ono in orange juice. When done, remove the fish from the marinade and blot dry. Coat with a mixture of flour, salt, tarragon, garlic powder, and pepper.

Saute:
To avoid crowding, cook the fish in 2 pans or batches. Saute in butter until light brown on both sides. When done, place the fish on a plate, and cover to keep warm. Keep the juices in the pan.

Saute and simmer 25 to 35 minutes:
In a clean saucepan, heat the orange juice over medium heat until reduced by 2/3. In the fish pan, over a hot flame, saute the shallots, ginger, and pineapple. Cook until the shallots are translucent.

Add the orange juice, passion fruit puree, and white wine to the fish pan and reduce until thick. Add the cream and simmer until reduced by half. Keep the sauce at a simmer while adding the butter. Add the butter piece by piece, whisking constantly until incorporated. Salt and pepper to taste.

Reheat the fish:
Return the fish to the glaze pan to rewarm and coat with glaze.

Serve:
Serve on warm plates covered with Pineapple-Passion Fruit Glaze. Garnish with tropical fruit.

Serves 6

WESTCOURT IN
THE BUTTES
TOP OF THE ROCK
Tempe
Chef Franklin Biggs

SEARED AHI TUNA WITH SHIITAKE MUSHROOMS AND SAUCE NATURELLE

6 Ahi Tuna, 6 oz. each
2T Shallots, ground
2T Garlic, ground
2C Shiitake Mushrooms, sliced
1C Fish Stock, recipe follows
1 bunch Parsley (1/4C chopped)
1T fresh Thyme
Garnish:
Fresh Thyme

Saute and simmer 10 minutes:
Place the tuna in a nonstick pan, with no butter or oil. Sear the tuna over a very hot flame, 2 minutes on each side. Remove the tuna. Reduce the heat to medium, and place the shallots, garlic, and mushrooms in the pan. Saute 2 minutes. Add the fish stock, parsley, and thyme, and heat until warm.

Serve:
Place the fish on a plate, pour the pan sauce on top, and garnish with fresh thyme.

Serves 6

FISH STOCK
A light and flavorful stock.

1 lb. Fish Bones and Scrap
1 Onion
1 bunch Parsley Stems
1 stick Celery
1T White Peppercorns
2C Cold Water

Simmer 1 hour. Strain.

LOEWS VENTANA CANYON RESORT
VENTANA ROOM

Tucson

Chef Takashi Shiramizu

176

CATFISH NEW ORLEANS

2C Flour
3 Eggs
1C Milk
2C Cornmeal
1t Cajun Spice
1/2t Garlic, granulated
1T Black Pepper
4 Catfish Filets, 8 oz. each
8T clarified Butter
1 medium Onion, chopped
2 Green Bell Peppers, chopped
1C sliced Mushrooms
2C Pouilly Fuisse*

*Pouilly Fuisse is a dry, white wine.

Coat:
Place flour in a bowl. In another bowl, beat the eggs and milk
together. In a third bowl, mix the cornmeal, cajun spice, garlic, and
pepper. Dip the filets in the flour, then in the egg mixture, then in
the cornmeal mixture.

Saute:
Saute the catfish over very high heat in butter. First saute 1 side.
Place the onion, green peppers, and mushrooms next to the catfish.
Turn the catfish and saute the other side. Reduce the heat to
medium, take the pan away from the stove, and add the wine. The
wine will ignite as you pour it into the pan. Return to the burner
and simmer for 2 minutes.

Serves 4

**BIG MAN'S
CATERING**
Kingman
Chef Watkin Sells

FRIED CATFISH WITH CREOLE MUSTARD SAUCE

Fish:
2 Catfish filets, 7 to 8 oz. each

Marinade:
2 Eggs, beaten
2t Cajun Spice, recipe below
2 Green Onions, chopped
1/2 Lemon, sliced thin
1/2C Half and Half
2T Worcestershire
1T Dijon Mustard

Bread Crumbs:
2C Bread Crumbs
2t Shallots, chopped
2t Garlic, chopped
1t Cajun Spice, recipe follows
1T Parsley, chopped
1T Parmesan Cheese
1T Olive Oil

Sauce:
Creole Mustard Sauce, recipe follows

Marinate 4 hours:
Place the catfish in a mixture of all marinade ingredients. Refrigerate.

Coat and brown:
Dip the filets in a mixture of all bread crumb ingredients. Brown the fish in oil on the stovetop. Drain the oil when done.

Bake 8 minutes at 450 degrees.

Serve:
Top the filets with Creole Mustard Sauce.

Serves 2

CAJUN SPICE

1T Cayenne
2t White Pepper
1T Black Pepper
2t Dry Mustard
2T Oregano, dried
2T Basil, dried
2T Thyme, dried
2T Fennel Seeds

Mix well.

Yields 3/4C

CREOLE MUSTARD SAUCE

1t Shallots, chopped
1t Garlic, chopped
1t Cajun Spice
1/4C Dry Sherry
1t Lemon Juice
1/2C Heavy Cream
1/4C Tomato Concasse
2 Green Onions, chopped
2t Dijon Mustard
2t Butter
Salt, to taste

Saute several minutes:
In a saute pan, cook the shallots, garlic, and cajun spice at full flame for a few seconds. Deglaze with sherry, and reduce to half volume. Add the lemon juice, cream, tomato concasse, green onions, and mustard. Saute for a few minutes until the sauce is thick enough to coat the back of a spoon, and the mustard is well blended. Add butter and salt.

DEJA VU
Lake Havasu City
Chef Carl Husbands

RED SNAPPER IN BEER DOUGH

1 Egg
4T Butter
3T Flour
1t Salt
1t White Pepper
1/4t Oregano
1T fresh Parsley, chopped
1/4C domestic Beer
1 pinch Nutmeg
2T Milk
4 Red Snapper Filets, 8 oz. each

Garnish:
Lemon wedge
Boiled Potatoes
Creamy Spinach

Coat:
In a large bowl, mix all ingredients except the snapper until a smooth dough forms. Turn the snapper in dough until totally covered.

Bake 10 to 15 minutes:
Preheat the oven to 400 degrees. Place the filets on a buttered baking sheet. Reduce the temperature to 350 degrees and bake until golden brown.

Serve:
Serve with a lemon wedge, boiled potatoes, and creamy spinach.

Serves 4

CHEZ RENE'S SWISS CHALET
Wickenburg
Chef Rene Lenggenhager

LINGUINE WITH SMOKED SALMON

8 oz. Linguine
2C Tomato Vodka Cream Sauce, recipe p. 51
4 oz. Smoked Salmon
1t Dill

Boil:
Cook the linguine.

Simmer several minutes:
Place the salmon and sauce in a skillet. Reduce by 1/3 over medium heat. Add the cooked linguine and dill, and toss.

Serves 2

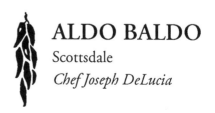

ALDO BALDO
Scottsdale
Chef Joseph DeLucia

GRILLED SALMON WITH TOMATO BASIL BUTTER SAUCE

4 fresh Salmon Filets, 7 oz. each, boneless
Tomato Basil Butter Sauce, recipe follows

Garnish:
See serving suggestions

Grill:
Grill the salmon over mesquite wood or charcoal until medium rare or desired doneness.

Serve:
Top with Tomato Basil Butter Sauce. This dish goes nicely with fresh vegetables and potato, rice, or pasta.

Serves 4

TOMATO BASIL BUTTER SAUCE

1T Garlic, crushed
1T Shallots, chopped
1 Bay Leaf
10 to 12 Black Peppercorns, whole
2C White Wine
1-1/2 qts. Heavy Cream
1-1/2 lb. Butter
3 fresh Tomatoes, chopped
2 bunches fresh Basil, chopped
Salt and Pepper, to taste
Fresh Lemon Juice, to taste

Heat 25-30 minutes total:
Place the garlic, shallots, bay leaf, peppercorns, and white wine in a

sauce pot. Bring to a boil, reduce heat, and simmer. Cook slowly until the liquid has nearly evaporated, 15 to 20 minutes. Add the cream and cook 10 to 12 minutes until the cream is reduced by half. Add the butter a little at a time, stirring constantly until well blended.

Add:
Remove from heat and strain. Add tomatoes, basil, salt, pepper, and lemon juice.

Serves 4 to 10

**LOS ABRIGADOS
CANYON ROSE**
Sedona
Chef Todd Hall

BRAISED SALMON WITH MINT AND SORREL TOMATO COULIS

Braised Salmon served with Vegetable Garnish and Fried Leek (see Side Dishes) makes a full meal. Prepare the garnish before the salmon.

> 4 Tomatoes, peeled, cores and seeds removed
> 28 oz. Salmon, cut into 4 pieces,
>   pin bones removed
> 4T Chicken Stock
> 8T Unsalted Butter
> 3 Shallots
> 2 cloves Garlic
> Salt, lightly to taste
> Fresh cracked White Pepper, lightly to taste
> 1t Mint, julienne
> 2T Sorrel, julienne

> **Garnish:**
> Vegetable Garnish, recipe p. 66
> Fried Leek, recipe p. 67

Blend:
Puree the tomatoes until smooth. Strain.

Bring to boil:
On the stovetop, place the pureed tomatoes, salmon, stock, butter, shallots, garlic, salt, and pepper in a large baking pan. Bring to a slow boil.

Bake 6 to 7 minutes:
Cover the fish pan with parchment paper or foil, place it in the oven, and bake at 400 degrees. When done, remove the fish from the pan and set the fish in a warm place. Keep the juices in the pan.

Simmer:
Place the fish pan on a stovetop burner, and add the mint and sorrel. Simmer over a hot flame until you reach your desired consistency. Mr. Stratta prefers the consistency of a watery puree.

Serve:
Lay the filets on 4 warm plates. Pour 4T sauce around each salmon. Arrange the vegetable garnish on the sauce, and set the fried leek on top of the fish.

Serves 4

THE PHOENICIAN
MARY ELAINE'S
Scottsdale
Chef Alessandro Stratta

OVEN POACHED DORADO WITH SHRIMP MOUSSE

Known in Mexico as dorado, this fish is better known by its Hawaiian name, mahi-mahi.

> 6 oz. Shrimp, peeled and deveined
> 1t Tomato Paste
> 1C Heavy Cream
> 1-1/2T Red Bell Pepper, roasted, peeled and diced
> 2T Green Onions, white only, finely chopped
> Salt and Pepper, to taste
> 6 Dorado filets, 5 oz. each
> 1-1/2C White Wine
> Grapefruit Sauce, recipe follows
>
> **Garnish:**
> Grapefruit wedges

Mix and stuff:
Puree the shrimp in a food processor. Slowly add the tomato paste and cream, and mix until well blended and fluffy. Fold in the bell pepper, onions, salt, and pepper. Slit a lengthwise pocket in the filets. Using a pastry bag or spoon, fill the pocket with stuffing.

Bake 12 minutes:
Place the fish on a baking tray and pour wine around the fish. Bake at 375 degrees until the mousse is firm.

Serve:
Ladle warm Grapefruit Sauce onto the dorado. Garnish with peeled grapefruit wedges.

Serves 6

GRAPEFRUIT SAUCE

Grapefruit sauce goes well with many foods, such as chicken breast or grilled fish. It is great for low salt or low fat diets.

3T Sugar
1T Grapefruit Zest, fine julienne
2T Shallots, chopped
3/4C White Wine
1/4C Tequila
Juice from 1 large Ruby Red Grapefruit*
Salt and White Pepper, to taste
2T Cornstarch or 1-3/4T Arrowroot
2-1/2T fresh Cilantro, chopped

*Use white grapefruit if red is unavailable.

Heat 15 minutes:
In a sauce pan over high heat, cook the sugar until it caramelizes. Add the grapefruit zest and shallots. Toss quickly for a moment. Add the wine and tequila. Boil 3 minutes. The sugar will crystallize. Add the grapefruit juice, salt, and pepper. Reduce heat to low, and simmer until the sugar dissolves. Stir in the cornstarch and bring to a boil, stirring until thickened. Lower the heat to warm. Keep the sauce warm, but watch to make sure it does not continue to thicken. If so, remove from heat or lower heat. Just

SOLARIUM
RESTAURANT
Tucson
Chef Jonathan Landeen

TUNA SCALLION FIESTA

1 can of Tuna, drained
2 Green Onions, chopped
1/4C Sour Cream
1 Tomato, diced
1t Salt
1t White Pepper
1t Rosemary
1t Dill
Dash of Tabasco

Garnish:
Tomato flower
Lime wedge
Paprika

Mix:
Mix the tuna, onions, sour cream, and tomato in a large mixing bowl until the tuna is broken up and creamy. Add the salt, pepper, rosemary, dill, and Tabasco. Mix well.

Refrigerate 2 to 4 hours.

Serve:
Serve the tuna in a tomato flower garnished with a lime wedge and paprika.

Serves 4

**THE
IMPECCABLE PIG**
Scottsdale
Chef Shane Taggart

SHRIMP AL'INDIANE

Shrimp Al'Indiane goes well with wild rice, glazed carrots, and chutney.

> 20 large Shrimp, raw, peeled
> 4T Chablis Wine
> 2T Shrimp Stock*
> 2T Indian Curry Powder
> 1t Salt
> 1t White Pepper
> 1/2t Garlic Powder
> 2 drops Tabasco
> 2T Butter
> 1T Flour
> 4T fresh Cream

> *To make shrimp stock, boil the shells 15 minutes in vegetable broth (onions, celery, bay leaves). Or substitute fish stock.

Saute few minutes:
Saute the shrimp, wine, and stock over medium heat until the shrimp turn pink. When done, remove the shrimp; keep the liquid in the pan.

Mix:
Add the curry powder, salt, pepper, garlic powder, and Tabasco to the reserved liquid. Mix well.

Saute and boil few minutes:
In another saute pan over medium-low flame, heat the butter and flour. Stir until well blended. Add the cream, stirring slowly as you add. Pour the mixture into the pan with the seasoned liquid, and bring to a boil. Stir constantly until the sauce is creamy.

Serve:
Place the shrimp on plate and pour the curry cream sauce on top.

**CHEZ RENE'S
SWISS CHALET**
Wickenburg
Chef Rene Lenggenhager

SHRIMP PUERTO PEÑASCO
Rocky Point Shrimp

Shrimp Puerto Peñasco originated near the rocky beaches of Puerto Peñasco, Mexico - famous for its shrimp fishing, tequila brewing, and tourist merriment. Chef Tompkins created the dish on the beach one night, cooking over an open fire. Despite its casual beginnings, Shrimp Puerto Peñasco is an elegant appetizer or the perfect light meal.

2C White Rice
1/4C White Wine
Pinch Saffron Threads
Pinch Salt
1T Canola Oil
24 large Gulf Shrimp, peeled and deveined
2 Jalapeño Peppers, deseeded and minced
2 cloves Garlic, minced
4T Tequila
2T White Wine
1T Honey
1/2T chopped, fresh Cilantro
1t Salt
1/2 lb. Unsalted Butter

Garnish:
2 Avocados, sliced

Simmer 20 minutes:
Place the rice, wine, saffron, and salt in a pot with enough water to cover the rice by 1 inch. Bring to a boil, reduce heat, cover, and simmer.

Saute and simmer several minutes:
Heat the oil in a large pan over medium-high heat. Add the shrimp and peppers, and cook for 3 minutes, turning the shrimp constantly. Add the garlic, tequila, and wine. Cook until nearly evaporated. Add the honey, cilantro, and salt. Simmer for 2 minutes, until the liquid is nearly evaporated. Stir in the butter.

Serve:
Lay the shrimp on a bed of rice. Garnish with sliced avocados.

Serves 4

THE
ARIZONA CLUB
Scottsdale
Chef Scott Tompkins

SHRIMP MARIE

2 Tomatoes, peeled and cut into 1/4 inch slices
Any Italian Vinaigrette with garlic
10 Jumbo Shrimp
1/2t Pesto, recipe below
5 oz. Alaskan King Crabmeat
5 slices Bacon
1/2t Butter
1/2t Garlic
8 oz. Spinach (16 leaves)
Salt and Pepper, to taste

Marinate:
Immerse the tomatoes in vinaigrette. Set aside.

Prepare the pesto:
Recipe below.

Fill the shrimp:
Peel, devein, and butterfly the shrimp. Fill each shrimp with 1/2t pesto and 1/2 oz. crab. Wrap each shrimp with 1/2 slice bacon.

Broil 6 to 8 minutes:
Place 5 shrimp on each of two skewers. Broil over an open flame or under a broiler until moist and tender.

Saute 3 minutes:
In a pot, over medium heat, saute the garlic in butter for 1 minute. Add the spinach, salt, and pepper. Cover and saute for 2 minutes. Drain.

Serve:
Arrange the spinach in the center of the plate, the tomatoes on the side, and the shrimp on top.

Serves 2

PESTO

1/2C fresh Basil, firmly packed, no stems
1/4C Italian Parsley, firmly packed, no stems
1/4C Parmesan Cheese, grated
1/4C Pine Nuts, chopped
1/8C Garlic, minced
1/8C Olive Oil

Puree until smooth.

Yields 2 Cups

MARRIOTT
MOUNTAIN SHADOWS
SHELLS
Scottsdale
Chef Christopher R. Klett

MARICOPA COUNTY SCAMPI

2 lbs. Shrimp, peeled and deveined
2-1/2C Rice or Rice Pilaf
8T Butter
1/4C Onion, finely chopped
1/4C Frog Leg meat
1C Heavy Cream
1t Salt
1t White Pepper
1t Oregano
1t Cloves
1/4C Brandy, optional
Cornstarch
2t Garlic, minced

Garnish:
Lemon

Steam 20 minutes:
Steam the rice.

Heat several minutes total:
Melt the butter in a medium saucepan over low heat. Set all but 3T aside. Raise the heat to medium. Add the onion and frog leg. Saute until fully cooked. Add the cream and slowly bring to a boil. Add the salt, pepper, oregano, cloves, and brandy. Thicken with cornstarch. Keep the sauce warm over low heat.

Saute:
In a large skillet over medium heat, saute the shrimp with the reserved butter and 2t garlic. The shrimp is done when it turns bright pink on the outside and white on the inside. Do not overcook.

Serve:
Place the shrimp on a nest of rice. Pour the sauce on top and garnish with lemon.

Serves 4

THE IMPECCABLE PIG
Scottsdale
Chef Shane Taggart

SCAMPI "VERA CRUZ"

3T Olive Oil
2 Cloves Garlic, minced
1/4C Onion, julienne
3 large red Tomatoes, peeled and diced
1/4C Green Chilies, julienne
1T Capers
1/4C Stuffed Green Olives, sliced
1/2t Thyme, fresh
1/2t Oregano, fresh
Juice and zest of 1 Orange
1t Sonoran Seasoning or Mexican Seasoning
1C Dry White Wine
1t Shallots
1-1/2 lbs. raw Shrimp, peeled and deveined

Garnish:
Lemon
Chopped Cilantro or Parsley
Rice, Tortilla, or Cumin Pepper Toast

Saute and simmer 15-20 minutes:
In a skillet, saute the garlic and onion in olive oil until soft. Add the tomatoes, chilies, capers, olives, thyme, oregano, orange juice and zest, and Sonoran Seasoning. Simmer 5 minutes. Add the wine and shallots. Simmer 5 more minutes. Add the shrimp, and gently simmer 5 minutes.

Serve:
Serve in a bowl over rice or accompanied by a grilled flour tortilla, cumin pepper toast, and lemon. Sprinkle with chopped cilantro or parsley.

Serves 4

SHERATON
TUCSON EL CONQUISTADOR
Tucson
Chef Alan Zeman

SCAMPI NAPOLITANA

4 servings Pasta
2 pats Butter
2 cloves Garlic, minced
12 to 15 Shrimp
1/4t Sweet Basil, dried
Tip of a teaspoon of Oregano, dried
Tip of a teaspoon of Marjoram, dried
Dash of Thyme, dried
3T Chardonnay
2C Marinara Sauce, recipe follows

Prepare:
Prepare the pasta and Marinara Sauce.

Saute and simmer few minutes:
Melt the butter in a saute pan. Add the garlic, shrimp, basil, oregano, marjoram, and thyme. Cook quickly over high heat until the shrimp turn pink. Reduce the heat; add the wine and Marinara Sauce. Simmer 1 minute.

Serve:
Serve over pasta.

Serves 4

MARINARA SAUCE

1/2C Olive Oil
1t chopped Garlic
1C Tomato Paste
2C Water
1t Oregano
2t Sweet Basil
1 Bay Leaf
Pinch of Thyme
Pinch of Rosemary
Pinch of Red Pepper
Dash of Salt

Saute and simmer 1 hour:
Saute the garlic in olive oil until the garlic is lightly browned. Add and blend the tomato paste and water. Add the seasonings. Bring to a boil, reduce heat to low, and simmer for an hour.

BIG MAN'S CATERING
Kingman
Chef Watkin Sells

SCAMPI
EL CONQUISTADOR

Shrimp:
16 Jumbo Shrimp, peeled and deveined
   and/or 2 petite Lobster Tails
1/2C Olive Oil
1/2C White Wine
1T Garlic, chopped

Sauce:
1T Shallots
1t Olive Oil
1/4C White Wine
2C Tomato Puree
1/2C Clam Juice
1t Chipotle Paste
1t Cilantro, chopped

Vegetables:
2C Frozen Kernel Corn, thawed
1/2C Black Beans
1 Red Bell Pepper
1 Green Chili Pepper
1t Cilantro

Garnish:
8 sheets Filo

PREPARATION

Soak overnight and simmer 2 hours:
Soak the beans overnight in warm water. Place the beans in a pot with enough fresh water to keep the beans covered. Bring to a boil, reduce heat to low, and simmer until the beans become tender.

Peel chili:
Peel and dice the chili. The Appendix describes several methods. The preferred method for this recipe is to broil until the skin turns black.

Bake filo fans:
Lightly oil the filo. Fold the sheets in half, then fold like a fan.Cut the fans in 2-inch lengths. Pinch one side, spread the other end open and oil lightly. Bake at 375 degrees for several minutes until lightly brown.

THE SCAMPI

Saute several minutes:
In a skillet, saute the shrimp in olive oil until the outside has just turned pink, and the inside turns white. Deglaze with 1/2C wine and garlic. Remove the shrimp. Keep the liquid in the pan.

Saute and simmer 20 minutes:
Place the shallots and 1t olive oil in the shrimp pan and saute until translucent. Add the wine and simmer for a few minutes. Add the tomato puree, clam juice, chipotle paste, and cilantro. Simmer 15 minutes. Strain.

In a separate pan, over medium high heat, saute the corn, peeled peppers, and cooked beans. Heat until the vegetables become hot. Add cilantro.

Serve:
Ladle sauce onto the center of 4 plates. Lay the vegetables on top. Place 4 shrimp around the perimeter of each plate with tails to the center. Set 2 filo fans on each.

Serves 4

SHERATON
TUCSON
EL CONQUISTADOR
Tucson
Chef Alan Zeman

SPAGHETTINI PORTOFINO

12 oz. Spaghettini
2T Olive Oil, heated
10 Bay Scallops
12 Rock Shrimp
1t Garlic
2T Onion
1C White Wine
2C Tomato
Salt and Pepper, to taste

Garnish:
Fresh Basil

Boil:
Cook the spaghettini to al dente, rinse and drain.

Saute and simmer 12 to 15 minutes:
Sear the olive oil, scallops, and shrimp over high heat until the shrimp turns white. Add the garlic and onion, and cook until translucent. Deglaze with wine 2 minutes. Add the tomato, salt, and pepper, and simmer 8 minutes.

Serve:
Toss the sauce and pasta. Place in pasta dishes, and garnish with basil leaves.

Serves 2

ALDO BALDO
Scottsdale
Chef Joseph DeLucia

GULF OF SIAM

1-1/2 to 2-1/2C Rice
1T Oil
4 to 6 Shrimp, medium sized
6 to 8 Calamari
2 White Fish filets, 10 inches each, cut into pieces
6 to 8 Scallops, medium sized
3 to 4 Mussels
1T Fish Sauce or 1/4T Salt
1T Oyster Sauce
1-1/2t Lemon Juice
1-1/2t Red Chili Paste
3/4t Garlic, chopped
3/8t White Pepper, ground
3/4t Cilantro
1/2C Tomato, chopped
1/2C Zucchini, chopped
1/3C Mushrooms, chopped
1/3C Green Bell Peppers, chopped
1/3C Red Bell Peppers, chopped

Steam 20 minutes:
Steam 2 to 4 servings of your favorite rice.

Saute 5 to 7 minutes:
Heat a wok over high flame. Add the oil and heat. Add the
remaining ingredients. Cook, stirring, until the scallops are done.

Serve:
Set the hot food on the steamed rice.

**PINK PEPPER
THAI CUISINE**
Scottsdale, Mesa, Phoenix
Chef Tony Tavee

PASTA SHELLFISH

Angel Hair Pasta, 2 servings
4 Mussels
4 Clams
4 Shrimp
8 Scallops
1/2C White Wine
4T Butter
1C Tomato Bouillon or Spaghetti Sauce
1/2T Sweet Red Pepper
1/2T Yellow Pepper
1/2T Scallions
1T Scampi Butter, recipe follows

Garnish:
French Bread

Boil:
Boil the pasta al dente, rinse and drain.

Prepare Scampi Butter:
Recipe follows.

Saute:
Saute the seafood, wine and butter over medium heat for a few minutes until half cooked. Add the bouillon and cook until the clams and mussels open.

In another pan, saute the cooked pasta, red pepper, yellow pepper, and scallions in butter until the peppers are slightly crispy.

Serve:
Ladle the pasta-vegetable mixture onto the middle of a plate. Slice 1 baguette of French bread. Place the slices between the mussels and clams, around the vegetables.

Serves 2

SCAMPI BUTTER

1 lb. Butter
2T Garlic
2T Parsley
2T White Wine

Whip:
With a beater, whip all the ingredients until soft. Store in your
refrigerator for use in other recipes.

**MARRIOTT
MOUNTAIN SHADOWS**
SHELLS
Scottsdale
Chef Christopher R. Klett

TABBULEH OF SEA SCALLOPS WITH CUCUMBERS AND TOMATOES IN LIME VINAIGRETTE

Tabbuleh:
1/2C Water
1/3C Bulghur Wheat
Salt and Pepper
2 medium Tomatoes, uniform 1/4 inch pieces
6 Scallions, finely chopped
2T fresh Mint, chopped
2T fresh Parsley, chopped
2T fresh Basil, chopped
Juice of 2 Limes
6T Extra Virgin Olive Oil
Salt and White Pepper, to taste

Topping:
Juice of 2 Limes
Salt and White Pepper, season lightly
1/2C Extra Virgin Olive Oil
1 large English Cucumber, peeled, seeded, fine julienne
2 medium Tomatoes, peeled, seeded, fine julienne
2T Chives, finely chopped
Salt and White Pepper, season lightly
1T Olive Oil
12 large fresh Scallops
Salt and Pepper, to taste

Bring to boil:
In a small pan, bring the water to a boil.

Mix and rest 10 to 15 minutes:
In a bowl or baking casserole, mix the bulghur, salt, and pepper. Add the boiling water. Cover, and set in a warm place, or very low oven, for 15 minutes until all the moisture is absorbed. The bulghur should be

soft and fluffy. If it is still hard after absorbing the water, add a little more boiling water, and let it be absorbed. Make sure the bulghur is not saturated, or it will become heavy and sticky. When done, keep at room temperature.

In a another bowl, combine the 2 diced tomatoes, scallions, mint, parsley, and basil. When the bulghur has cooled to room temperature, add this mixture to the bulghur and mix well. Add the lime juice, olive oil, salt, and pepper. Mix well. Adjust seasonings to taste.

Chill the tabbuleh.

Mix:
In a new bowl, mix the lime juice, salt, and pepper. Slowly add the olive oil. The vinaigrette does not need to emulsify.

In another bowl, combine the cucumber, 2 julienne tomatoes, chives, salt, and pepper.

Saute few minutes:
Just before serving, heat the olive oil in a thick bottom saute pan until smoking hot. Saute the scallops, salt, and pepper until dark brown on both sides. Remove from pan.

Serve:
Put the tabbuleh in a ring or round mold. Gently set the tabbuleh in the center of a plate and remove the mold. Pass the cucumber and tomato garnish through the vinaigrette, and arrange around the tabbuleh. Cut the warm sea scallops in half, crosswise, and set them in a fan shape on the tabbuleh, alternating brown and white. Serve immediately.

Serves 4

THE PHOENICIAN
MARY ELAINE'S
Scottsdale
Chef Alessandro Stratta

FETTUCINE WITH SCALLOPS AND SHIITAKE MUSHROOMS

6 oz. Fettucine
2T Unsalted Butter
2 cloves Garlic, minced
4T Green Onions, sliced thin
3 oz. Shiitake Mushrooms,
   stems removed, sliced thin
6 oz. Scallops, whole
6T Sherry Wine
4t Dijon Mustard
6T Whipping Cream
4t Fresh Dill, chopped
Salt and White Pepper, to taste

Boil:
Boil the fettucine. The pasta may be cooked ahead of time and reheated later.

Saute and simmer 10 to 12 minutes:
In a saucepan, over medium-high flame, saute the butter, garlic, onions, mushrooms, and scallops 1 minute. Add the sherry and reduce by half. When just done, remove the scallops and set aside. Add the mustard and cream to the pan. Cook until the sauce begins to thicken. Add the dill, salt, and pepper. Cook for a moment. Return the scallops to the pan and heat thoroughly.

Serve:
Toss the scallops and mushrooms with the fettucine.

Serves 2

KEATON'S
RESTAURANT, GRILL AND BAR
Tucson

BUDDY'S GRILL
Tucson

BUSTER'S
RESTAURANT
Scottsdale and Flagstaff
Chef Tom Firth

SEAFOOD LINGUINE

2 servings of Linguine
8T Butter
2T Garlic (6 cloves, minced)
1/2C Crabmeat, flaked
1/4C Parmesan Cheese
1/4C Madeira Wine
1/2C Half and Half or Heavy Cream
6 large Shrimp, peeled and deveined

Boil:
Boil the linguine al dente, rinse and drain.

Saute and simmer 23 minutes:
Saute the butter and garlic over medium heat 3 minutes. Add the crab, cheese, wine, and cream. Simmer 15 minutes. Add the shrimp and simmer 3-6 minutes. If you prefer a thicker sauce, add more Parmesan cheese.

Serve:
Pour the seafood over the linguine.

**MICHAEL'S
FINE DINING**
Page
Chef Michael J. Decker

ANGEL HAIR PASTA, FRESH ARIZONA ESCARGOT IN A GARLIC CREAM SAUCE

Escargot:
10 oz. Angel Hair Pasta
25 fresh Arizona Escargot
4T White Wine
1/2C Celery, diced
1/2C Onion, minced
1/4t Thyme
1 Bay Leaf
2 Cloves, whole
Pinch of Salt

Sauce:
1t Unsalted Butter
5 cloves Garlic, minced
1 small Shallot, minced
3C Whipping Cream
Salt, to taste
White Pepper, to taste

Garnish:
Chopped Parsley

Let sit 2 to 3 hours:
Let the escargot sit in cold water. Change the water occasionally. Then rinse several times to rid the escargot of the slick coating.

Blanch:
Immerse the escargot in boiling water for a moment.

Simmer 1-1/2 hours:
Simmer the escargot in 3C water, wine, celery, onion, thyme, bay leaf, cloves, and salt. When done, discard the broth.

Remove shells:
Remove the escargot shells with pliers.

Saute and simmer 25 minutes:
Melt butter in a heavy, medium size saucepan over low heat. Add the garlic and shallot. Saute 2 minutes. Add the escargot and saute 2 more minutes. Remove the escargot with a slotted spoon. Set in a warm place. Add cream to the pan and cook until slightly thickened, about 20 minutes. Season with salt and pepper.

Boil:
Boil the pasta until just tender, stirring occasionally.

Serve:
Strain the sauce, through a fine sieve, over the pasta. Arrange 5 escargot around the pasta, and garnish with chopped parsley.

Serves 5

THE
MANSION CLUB
Phoenix
Chef Peter Inauen

LOBSTER SAVANNAH

2C Rice
4 Australian Lobster Tails, 8 oz. each
8T clarified Butter
1/2C Scallions, chopped
1/2C Shallots, chopped
1/4C Pimentos
1t Sweet Basil, dried
1 clove Garlic, chopped
1/2C Parsley, chopped
Pinch of Thyme
1C White Wine
2C Mornay Sauce, recipe p.165
Bearnaise Sauce, recipe follows

Steam 20 minutes:
Steam the rice.

Boil 2 to 3 minutes:
Remove the meat from the lobster shells. Set the meat aside. You will saute it later. Boil the shells until they turn orange. The orange shells make an attractive garnish.

Prepare the sauces.

Saute and simmer several minutes:
Over medium heat, saute the lobster meat, scallions, shallots, pimentos, sweet basil, garlic, parsley, and thyme in butter. Cook until the lobster turns white. Add the wine and Mornay Sauce. Heat and stir until well blended.

Serve:
Place a bed of rice on a plate and set a shell on top. Fill the shell with the lobster mixture, and add Bearnaise Sauce.

Serves 4

BEARNAISE SAUCE

1/2C White Wine
2T Tarragon Vinegar
1T Shallots, finely chopped
2 Peppercorns, crushed
2 sprigs Tarragon, chopped
1 sprig Chervil, finely chopped
3 Egg Yolks
3/4C Butter, melted

Heat 20 minutes:
Place the wine, vinegar, shallots, peppercorns, tarragon, and chervil in a double boiler. Heat until reduced by half. Cool. Return to the double boiler. Add the egg yolks, whisking constantly until thick. Remove from heat and add the butter a little at a time.

Yields 1-1/2 Cups

BIG MAN'S CATERING
Kingman
Chef Watkin Sells

BLUE CORN CRUSTED CHILE RELLENO WITH LOBSTER AND ORANGE CHIPOTLE CREAM SAUCE

Winner of the annual Southwest Mexican Cookoff Gold Medal.

2 Australian Lobster Tails
6 whole Anaheim Chilies
1/4 Red Bell Pepper
1/4 Yellow Sweet Pepper
Tomato Salsa, recipe follows
Orange Chipotle Cream Sauce, recipe follows
1/2C Jalapeño Jack Cheese, shredded
1/2 bunch Cilantro, chopped
1T Black Pepper
2T Heavy Whipping Cream
Flour
3 Eggs, beaten with 3T Milk
Blue Corn Breading or regular Cornmeal

Garnish:
Cilantro
Baby Cherry Tomatoes

Roast, peel and deseed:
Roast, peel and deseed the peppers. If you do not have salsa in stock, it will save time to roast and peel those peppers now. (Directions for roasting and peeling peppers can be found in the Appendix).
Roasting over an open flame is the preferred method for this recipe. To remove seeds from the 6 Anaheim chilies to be stuffed, make an incision on one side and scrape out the seeds. Deseed and dice the remaining peppers.

Prepare the sauces:
Recipes follow.

Boil 8 minutes:
Boil the lobster tails. Remove the shells and chop the meat.

Stuff and coat:
Mix the lobster, cheese, red pepper, yellow pepper, cilantro, black pepper, and whipping cream by hand. Stuff the roasted chilies with the mixture. Dip the chilies in flour, then in the egg mixture, and then in the breading.

Fry:
Deep fry or pan fry the chilies. To pan fry, heat oil over a medium flame. The oil should be deep enough to cover the chilies half way. Add the chilies. When brown on 1 side, turn over and brown the other side.

Serve:
Pour Orange Chipotle Cream Sauce onto the base of each plate. Sprinkle Tomato Salsa over the cream sauce. Cut the chilies open and lay them on top of the salsa. Garnish with cilantro, fresh baby cherry tomatoes, and the reserved chipotle sauce.

Serves 6

TOMATO SALSA

    2 large, ripe Tomatoes, seeded and diced
    1/4 Onion, diced
    2 cloves Garlic, minced
    1 Anaheim Chile, roasted and diced
    1/2 Yellow Sweet Pepper, roasted and diced
    1/2 Red Bell Pepper, roasted and diced
    1/2 bunch Cilantro, chopped
    Salt and Pepper, to taste

Combine. Serve at room temperature.

(continued on next page)

ORANGE CHIPOTLE CREAM SAUCE

> 1 qt. Orange Juice
> 2 Chipotle Chilies
> Light Cream Sauce, recipe follows

Simmer 20 to 25 minutes:
Cook the orange juice and chilies over moderate heat until the liquid is reduced by half. Remove 6T for garnishing chile rellenos. Add the cream sauce to the remainder and mix.

LIGHT CREAM SAUCE

> 2 Shallots, chopped
> 2T Ventana Chardonnay
> 1C Heavy Cream
> 1T Roux

Simmer 5 minutes:
Cook the shallots, chardonnay, and cream over moderate heat 4 minutes. Slowly add the roux and blend.

LOEWS VENTANA CANYON RESORT
VENTANA ROOM
Tucson
Chef Tim Fields

VEGETARIAN

Ravioli of Fresh Black Truffles
Spinach and Wild Mushroom Strudel with
  Garlic Parmesan Cream
Spanikopites
Gnocchi Avanti
Orzo with Fresh Herbs and Lemon Buerre Blanc
Spinach Ravioli with Tomato Vodka Cream Sauce
Blue Corn Cheesy Enchiladas
Revithosalata

RAVIOLI OF FRESH BLACK TRUFFLES

Ravioli can also be prepared with other fresh, fine wild mushrooms.

    2-1/4C Flour
    Fine Sea Salt, to taste
    Fresh ground White Pepper, to taste
    2 Eggs
    3 Egg Yolks
    1/2t Truffle Oil*
    1/2t Extra Virgin Olive Oil
    1 oz. fresh Black Truffles, thinly sliced
    1t Olive Oil
    4T dry Champagne
    2 Pearl Onions, thinly sliced*
    1/2 medium Carrot, thinly sliced
    4 oz. Whipped Cream, stiff
    4T Unsalted Butter
    Salt and Pepper to taste

    Garnish:
    Chervil

    *Truffle oil can be purchased in gourmet markets.
     Pearl onions are mild onions.

Blend:
In a food processor, blend the following ingredients in the order listed: flour, salt, pepper, eggs, egg yolks, truffle oil, and olive oil. Blend until the dough starts to form a ball. The dough should be stiff enough to hold its shape when standing alone. If the dough is too wet, add more flour. If too dry, add more yolks. When finished, wrap the dough in a towel or wax paper.

Let sit 30 minutes.

Form ravioli:
Use a rolling pin or pasta machine to roll the dough as thin as possible. Cut the pasta into 4-inch diameter circles or squares. Place 3 truffle slices on each pasta square. Save the remaining truffles for the sauce. Lightly moisten the pasta edges with water. Fold the pasta around the truffles and pinch closed.

Boil 2 minutes:
Cook the ravioli in boiling water with a little olive oil.

Heat few minutes:
Reduce the reserved truffles, champagne, onions, and carrot by 3/4 over moderate heat. Add the whipped cream, butter, salt, and pepper. Bring to a quick boil.

Serve:
Pour sauce around the ravioli and garnish with chervil.

Serves 4

CHRISTOPHER'S
Phoenix
Chef Christopher Gross

SPINACH AND WILD MUSHROOM STRUDEL WITH GARLIC PARMESAN CREAM

Clarified Butter or Vegetable Oil, to coat pan
2T Garlic, finely minced
2T Shallot, finely minced
1/2C White Onion, finely chopped
1C Mushrooms, finely chopped*
1/2C Pernod Liqueur*
2C Heavy Cream
1-1/2C Parmesan Cheese, freshly grated
1 lb. frozen Spinach, thawed, water squeezed out
1t Dry Mustard
Salt and Pepper, to taste
6 sheets Filo Dough
1C Clarified Butter
Garlic Parmesan Cream, recipe follows

Garnish:
Tomato, diced
Spinach Leaves

*Use any combination of oyster, shiitake, or white
 domestic mushrooms. Pernod is an anise liqueur.

Saute and simmer 12 to 18 minutes:
Saute the garlic, shallot, onion, and mushrooms in butter over
medium heat. Add the liqueur and flame for 30 seconds. Add the
heavy cream and reduce by half. Whisk in the Parmesan cheese.

Cool to room temperature.

Mix:
In a large bowl, use your hands to mix the mushroom-cream mixture,
spinach, mustard, salt, and pepper.

Assemble the strudel:
Brush the filo with butter, and lay the sheets on top of each other so both sides become buttered. Place each filo sheet on wax paper and spread the spinach filling evenly along the narrow end. Roll tightly like a jelly roll, using the edge of the wax paper as a guide. Wrap in wax paper.

Refrigerate overnight.

Bake 15 to 20 minutes:
Remove the wax paper, and place the rolls on an ungreased baking sheet. Bake at 375 degrees until evenly browned.

Let rest 10 to 15 minutes.

Serve:
Cover the bottom of a plate with Garlic Parmesan Cream. Using a very sharp knife, cut the strudel into 1 inch thick slices. Overlap the slices along the bottom edge of the plate. Garnish with finely diced tomato and fresh spinach leaf.

Serves 4

GARLIC PARMESAN CREAM

Clarified Butter or Vegetable Oil, to coat pan
2T Garlic, finely minced
2C Heavy Cream
3/4C Parmesan Cheese, freshly grated
Salt and Pepper, to taste

Saute and simmer 12 to 18 minutes:
Saute the garlic in butter over medium heat. Add the cream and reduce by half. Whisk in the cheese, salt, and pepper.

Yields 1-1/2C

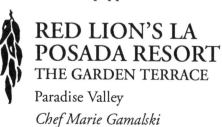

RED LION'S LA POSADA RESORT
THE GARDEN TERRACE
Paradise Valley
Chef Marie Gamalski

219

SPANAKOPITES
Spinach and Cheese Phyllo Triangles

Don't be misled by the length of this recipe. Forming spanakopites is actually quite easy. It just takes a bit of explanation - and the results are fabulous. Two methods of presentation are described below. The first tells how to form small triangles which can be served as a main course or as appetizers for parties. The second is much quicker. The Spanikopite is formed in layers, like lasagne. It should be served immediately.

Spanakopites can be prepared a week in advance, and stored in the refrigerator until ready for baking. We do not suggest freezing either cooked or uncooked, although some commercially made spanakopites are shipped frozen.

> 4 bunches fresh Spinach, washed several times
> 1/4C Olive Oil
> 1-1/2 medium Onions, finely chopped
> 2 Leeks, finely chopped
> 1 bunch fresh Dill, chopped
> 1 lb. Feta Cheese, crumbled
> 1/2C Kefalotyri Cheese, grated*
> 1t freshly ground Pepper
> 1t freshly ground Nutmeg
> 2 Eggs, beaten*
> 1/2C Butter, melted (or Margarine and/or Olive Oil)
> 1/2 lb. Phyllo Pastry

*Kefalotyri Cheese is a hard Greek cheese. If not available, substitute Parmesan. Eggs help bind the filling. If you are watching cholesterol, you may omit them without changing much flavor.

Steam 3 minutes:

Steam the spinach for 3 minutes until the leaves become limp but are still bright green. If steaming is not convenient, boil water in a stock pot, and place the spinach a little at a time into the boiling water. Let it cook for a moment until the leaves have just wilted.

Drain:

Immediately place the spinach in a colander and cover with ice to stop cooking. Let the spinach drain and cool.

Saute few minutes:

In a pot, heat the olive oil over medium heat. Add the onions and leeks, and saute until translucent and wilted. Remove from heat and cool to room temperature.

Chop:

Squeeze the spinach in your hands to remove as much water as possible. Otherwise the mixture will be too moist, and the phyllo will break during cooking. When the spinach is squeezed, cross-cut it into small pieces.

Mix:

Stir the chopped spinach and dill into the onions and leeks. Add the kefalotyri, egg, pepper, and nutmeg. Mix. Fold in the feta.

Prepare to work with phyllo:

The trick to working successfully with phyllo is organization and speed. Working at a long counter is helpful. To make triangles, you will need two baking sheets - one to work on, and one to put the spanikopites on. Place the phyllo on your left, the working sheet in the middle, and the baking sheet on the right. To make full-size portions, you just need one baking sheet.

(If you will not cook the spanikopites now, place wax paper strips on the right baking sheet. When done forming the spanikopites, lift them off the sheet and wrap them in wax paper for refrigeration.)

(continued on next page)

Open the phyllo carefully. Once the phyllo is open, work quickly. If it dries out, it will break, and be difficult to fold.

Form spanakopites - triangle method:
Cut the phyllo in half lengthwise. Place the halves on top of each other. Set one phyllo half sheet on the working tray. Fold it in half lengthwise. With a brush, lightly butter the top. Place a mound of spinach mixture (just over soup spoon-size) on top of one end of the folded phyllo.

Starting at the end with the mixture, fold one corner over the filling to form a triangle of equal sides. Do not add more filling. Fold again to make another triangle, and continue folding triangles until you get to the end of the strip.

Butter the top and bottom of the final triangle and place it on the right baking sheet. Repeat the process for each spanikopite.

Form spanikopites - lasagne method:
This method takes one-tenth the time as forming triangles. Don't cut the phyllo. Butter a baking sheet. Lay 2 full sheets of phyllo on the baking sheet. Lightly butter the top. Remove 2 more sheets of phyllo, butter them, and lay them on top of the first. Continue until you have layered 10 sheets of phyllo. Spread filling across the length of the sheets. Repeat the phyllo layers on top of the filling, again buttering after every 2 sheets, until you have layered 10 sheets. Push the sides in, and butter the top. Slightly cut serving-sized spanikopite (do not cut all the way through) into 4 pieces by 8 pieces.

Bake 8 to 15 minutes:
Bake at 450 degrees until just golden. Do not allow the phyllo to brown. The triangles should bake 8 to 10 minutes; full size spanikopite require 10 to 15 minutes.

Serves 15

GREEKFEST
Phoenix
Chef Tony Makridis

GNOCCHI AVANTI

3 boiling Potatoes, cut into cubes
1 lb. Ricotta Cheese
4 Eggs
2C Flour
2C Parmesan Cheese
Salt and Pepper, to taste
Tomato, Meat or Alfredo Sauce, recipe p.15

Boil and mash:
Boil the potatoes until tender. Peel the boiled potatoes and pass them through a potato ricer or mash them.

Knead:
Mix the potatoes, Ricotta, eggs, flour, Parmesan, salt, and pepper. Knead gently for 5 minutes.

Form gnocchi:
Cut the dough into several pieces, and roll each piece into a long, thin tube, resembling a cigar, 1/2 inch in diameter. Cut each roll into 1 inch segments. Lay the segments in a flour-dusted dish.

Boil for a few minutes:
Boil salted water in a large stock pot. Drop the gnocchi, one by one, into the pot. Stir lightly to prevent them from sticking to the bottom. In a few minutes, the gnocchi will rise to the surface. Let them cook another 30 seconds, then remove with a strainer.

Serve:
Serve the gnocchi with tomato, meat, or Alfredo sauce.

Serves 10

AVANTI
Phoenix, Scottsdale
Chef Angelo Livi

ORZO WITH FRESH HERBS AND LEMON BUERRE BLANC

1C Orzo, uncooked*
Lemon Buerre Blanc, recipe below
2-1/4t fresh Rosemary
2-1/4t fresh Thyme
2-1/4t fresh Sage
2-1/4t fresh Tarragon

*Orzo is a rice shaped pasta.

Prepare:
Boil the orzo until al dente. Rinse and drain. Prepare the Lemon Buerre Blanc. Chop and combine the herbs.

Serve:
Fold the herbs and Lemon Buerre Blanc into warm orzo.

Serves 4

LEMON BUERRE BLANC

1/2C Chablis
1/2C Rice Wine Vinegar
2 Bay Leaves
10 Peppercorns, cracked
2T Shallots, finely chopped
2C Heavy Cream
12 oz. Sweet Butter, softened and cubed
Juice from 4 fresh Lemons
Salt and Pepper, to taste

Heat 15 to 20 minutes:
Combine the chablis, vinegar, bay leaves, peppercorns, and shallots in a saucepan. Bring to a boil and reduce by half. Add the cream and reduce by half.

Add:
Remove from heat and whisk in the butter, a little at a time. Add the lemon juice, salt, and pepper.

RED LION'S LA POSADA RESORT
THE GARDEN TERRACE
Paradise Valley
Chef Marie Gamalski

SPINACH RAVIOLI WITH TOMATO VODKA CREAM SAUCE

12 Spinach Ravioli
2C Tomato Vodka Cream Sauce, recipe p.51
Garnish:
Tomato, diced
Parmesan Cheese

Boil and heat:
Boil the ravioli until done. Heat the sauce.

Serve:
Top with diced tomato and Parmesan cheese.

Serves 2

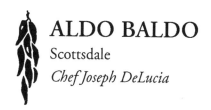

ALDO BALDO
Scottsdale
Chef Joseph DeLucia

BLUE CORN
CHEESY ENCHILADAS

1 doz. Blue Corn Tortillas, 6-inch diameter
1C Green Chili, diced
1/2C Onion, diced
1/2C Corn
1/2C Zucchini, diced
1C Refried Beans*
1/2C Enchilada Sauce
1/2 bunch fresh Cilantro, chopped (1/2C)
1T fresh Garlic, chopped
1t Chili Powder
1/4t Cumin
2-1/2C Cheddar, grated
1/2C Enchilada Sauce
1/2C Cheddar, grated

Garnish:
Sour Cream
Guacamole or sliced Avocado

*Feel free to experiment with filling ingredients. For example, you can substitute refried beans with cooked black beans, garbanzos, lentils, or 1/2C dry falafel cooked in 3/4C water for 5 minutes.

Warm:
Warm the tortillas in a frying pan with a very light coat of oil until they become soft..

Fill the tortillas:
In a bowl, mix all but the last 2 ingredients. Place 1/2 cup of filling on each tortilla. Roll the tortillas.

Bake 30 minutes:
Grease a 9-inch square baking pan, and spread 2T enchilada sauce on the bottom of the pan. Arrange the enchiladas in the pan, and top with 1/2C enchilada sauce and 1/2C cheddar cheese. Bake at 350 degrees.

Serve:
Serve with sour cream and guacamole or sliced avocado.

Serves 6

MACY'S
EUROPEAN COFFEEHOUSE
AND BAKERY
Flagstaff
Chef Sue-Bug Skelton

REVITHOSALATA
Chick-Pea Pâté

The Greek dining style is to order several appetizers and eat for hours. Light, nutritious, and full of flavor, Revithosalata can be served as an appetizer, as a light lunch, or with other dishes to make a feast.

3C raw fresh Chick-peas*
1T Baking Soda
2-1/2T Tahini
10 cloves fresh Garlic
1t Salt or Kosher Salt
1-1/4t Freshly ground Black Pepper
1-1/4t Freshly ground Coriander
3T Olive Oil*
1/4C Lemon Juice, freshly squeezed

Garnish:
Paprika
Fresh flat leaf Parsley
Kalamata Olives
Warm Bread or Pita Bread wedges

*Chick-peas are also called garbanzos. If you use canned chick-peas, do not soak, simmer or remove the husks. Cold pressed agoureleo is the preferred olive oil.

Let sit overnight:
Rinse the chick-peas in water. Let the chick-peas sit in baking soda overnight. When done, rinse and drain.

Simmer 1 hour:
Put the chick-peas in a pot, cover with water, and bring to a boil. Lower the heat, and simmer until tender.

Remove the husks:
Drain the chick-peas and cover them with icy water until they are cool. Take them out of the water and and rub a handful at a time to loosen the husks. Place the chick-peas in more cold water. The husks will rise to the top. Discard the husks and drain the chick-peas.

Blend 10 minutes:
Place the tahini, garlic, salt, pepper, and coriander in a food processor. Blend 5 minutes. Add the following ingredients one at a time, in the order listed, blending after each addition: the chick-peas, oil, lemon juice (add very slowly), and about 1/4C water (just enough to reach desired consistency). Blend 5 more minutes, until the revithosalata becomes creamy.

Chill.

Serve:
Place the revithosalata on a serving plate. Sprinkle with paprika and chopped fresh flat leaf parsley, and surround with kalamata olives. If desired, top with 1/2 to 1t olive oil. Serve with bread or warm pita bread wedges.

Yields 3-1/4C

GREEKFEST
Phoenix
Chef Tony Makridis

DESSERTS

Margarita Lime Pie
Apple Crostata
Peach Lemon Tart
Chocolate Tart
Chocolate Kahlua Silk Torte
  with Oreo Crust
Pralines and Cream Torte
Chocolate Chestnut Cake
Cheesecake
Pumpkin Cheesecake
Cranberry Nautical
Souffle Grand Marnier
Flourless Chocolate
  Souffle Cake
Nougat Glaciers

Parnassienne de Mousse
  au Chocolat
Spring in the Desert
Cassis Mousse wrapped in
  White Chocolate with
  Hazelnut and Chocolate
  Sauces
Cornbread Pudding with
  Sweet Nutmeg Cream
Strawberries Daniel with
  Dessert Crepes
Crepe Suzette
Kolachie
Tortoni
Chocolate Mint Ice Cream
Prickly Pear Sorbet

MARGARITA LIME PIE

1-1/4C to 2C Almonds, finely chopped
1/4C Sugar
1/4 to 1/3C Butter, melted
1C Sweetened Condensed Milk
3/4C fresh Lime Juice
6T Tequila
2 Egg Yolks
Garnish:
Whipped Cream
Lime slices
Toasted Almonds

Mix:
Combine the almonds, sugar, and butter.

Bake 5 minutes:
Line a pie tin with buttered aluminum foil. Press the above mixture to the bottom and sides of the tin. Bake at 425 degrees until light brown.

Mix:
Mix the milk, lime juice, tequila, and yolks.

Bake 35 minutes:
Pour the filling into the shell and bake at 350 degrees.

Chill overnight.

Serve:
Turn the pie upside down, peel off the foil, and return the pie to the tin. Decorate with whipped cream, lime slices, and toasted almonds.

Yields 1 Pie

THE BOULDERS RESORT
LATILLA RESTAURANT
Carefree
Chef Brent E. Wertz

APPLE CROSTATA

1-1/4C Flour
1/4C Margarine, softened
1/4C Sherry
3/4C Sugar
1C Sour Cream
1T Flour
1t Vanilla Extract
1 Egg, beaten
6 Apples, sliced and peeled
2/3C Flour
1/2C Sugar
1t Cinnamon
4 oz. Butter

Form the crust:
Mix the flour, margarine, and sherry. Roll out the dough and lay it in a 9-inch pie pan.

Mix the filling:
Place 3/4C sugar, sour cream, flour, vanilla and egg in a bowl. Mix well. Add the apples.

Mix the topping:
Mix 2/3C flour, 1/2C sugar, cinnamon, and butter until crumbly.

Bake 60 minutes:
Pour the filling in the pie shell and bake 45 minutes at 350 degrees. Add the topping and bake another 15 minutes.

Cool.

Yields 1 pie

SCORDATO'S
RESTAURANT
Tucson
Chef Jim Scordato

PEACH LEMON TART

Puff Pastry
Parchment Paper
3 Egg Yolks
3 Eggs
Juice and zest of 3 Lemons
1-1/2 oz. Sugar
8T Butter, softened, cut into small pieces
6 Peaches, medium sized
Melted Butter, to taste

Form shell:
Line an 11 x 1 inch tart pan with puff pastry. Line the pastry with parchment paper. Use beans, salt or anything heavy to fill the shell. The weight will prevent the pastry from puffing and losing the tart pan shape during cooking.

Bake 15 minutes:
Bake at 400 degrees. When done, remove the paper and weight.

Heat and whip 15 minutes:
Cook the egg yolks, eggs, lemon juice, and zest over a double boiler 15 minutes. As you cook, whip continuously until the mixture develops the consistency of mayonnaise. Remove from heat.

Whip:
While still warm, add the sugar and 4 oz. butter. Whip to blend.

Broil 10 minutes:
Cut the peaches in half, and brush with melted butter. Broil the peaches skin side up. When done, peel off the skin. Align the peaches in the puff pastry shell. Cover with lemon filling. Broil for a moment until brown. Watch to make sure it broils evenly.

Serves 8

DEJA VU
Lake Havasu City
Chef Carl Husbands

CHOCOLATE TART

5T Unsalted Butter
2-1/2 oz. Semi-sweet Chocolate Chips
2 Eggs
6T Sugar
1/4C Pastry Flour

Melt and mix:
Melt the butter and chocolate chips in a double boiler. In a bowl, whip the eggs and sugar together until they reach ribbon consistency. Combine and fold both mixtures. Add the flour. Cool.

Bake 4 minutes:
Pipe or spoon 2T mixture into each of 6 baking cups (cupcake size). Bake at 350 degrees until 3/4 done. The center should be shiny and slightly liquid.

Serve:
Trim the tarts in half vertically so they look like half moons. Serve with coffee.

Yields 12 Tarts

CHRISTOPHER'S
Phoenix
Chef Christopher Gross

CHOCOLATE KAHLUA SILK TORTE WITH OREO CRUST

7 Oreo Cookies, cream removed
4T Butter, melted
2T Cocoa Powder
12 oz. Butter, softened
12 oz. Light Corn Syrup
9 oz. Semi-sweet Chocolate, melted
6 Eggs
6T Kahlua
1T Instant Coffee dissolved in 2T warm water
1T Cocoa Powder
2C Cream, whipped
2T Kahlua

Mix:
In a food processor, crumble the Oreos until very fine. Add the butter and 2T cocoa powder and mix on low speed for 1 minute.

Form crust:
Line the bottom of a 10-inch spring form pan with a wax paper circle. Pack the crumb mixture in the pan to form a crust.

Mix:
In a mixer, cream the butter for 10 minutes. Add corn syrup and mix at medium speed. Add the following ingredients and mix at low speed, mixing and scraping the bowl after each addition: half the chocolate, the rest of the chocolate, the eggs (one at a time), 6T Kahlua, coffee, and 1T cocoa powder.

Chill 2 hours:
Pour the filling onto the crust and smooth off the top. Chill.

Top:
Top the torte with a mixture of whipped cream and 2T Kahlua.

Yields 1 Torte

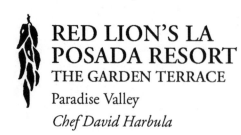

RED LION'S LA POSADA RESORT
THE GARDEN TERRACE
Paradise Valley
Chef David Harbula

PRALINES'N CREAM TORTE

1/2C Sugar
6T Water
Pinch Cream of Tartar
1C Pecans
1 lb. White Chocolate
8 oz. Butter
14 Eggs, separated
Whipped Cream

Garnish:
Toasted Pecans

Heat few minutes:
In a saucepan, over high heat, cook the sugar, water and cream of tartar until the sugar is a dark honey color. Stir in the pecans.

Grind:
Pour the praline mixture into a greased pan and cool. Grind in a food processor until fine.

Melt and mix:
Melt the white chocolate and butter in a saucepan. Whip the egg yolks until they become pale yellow. Whip the egg whites until they are firm but not dry.
Fold the whipped egg yolks into the chocolate mixture. Then fold in the egg whites. Fold in the pralines.

Bake 40 minutes:
Pour the batter into 2 greased 9-inch cake pans. Bake at 300 degrees until the center is firm and no longer jiggles when the pan is shaken.

Cool.

Top:
Ice with whipped cream and garnish with toasted pecans.

Serves 12

SHERATON
TUCSON
EL CONQUISTADOR
Tucson
Chef Christine Dettloff

CHOCOLATE CHESTNUT CAKE

8 oz. Semi-sweet Chocolate
1/4C Coffee, brewed
10 Egg Yolks
1C Sugar
2/3C Chestnut Puree*
10 Egg Whites
1/4C Sugar

4-6 oz. Semi-sweet Chocolate
2-3T Coffee, brewed
1-1/2C Heavy Whipping Cream
1-2T Orange flavored Liqueur or Rum

*Chestnut puree, sometimes called marrons, can be purchased in gourmet stores. Almond paste makes an excellent substitute. It has similar texture, but will change the flavor to almond.

THE CAKE

Melt:

Melt 8 oz. chocolate and 1/4C coffee in a double boiler. Cool to room temperature.

Mix:

In a mixer, beat the egg yolks, 1C sugar, and chestnut puree 6-8 minutes at high speed. Beat until light and fluffy. Fold in the melted chocolate mixture.

In another bowl, whip the egg whites at high speed. Whip until soft peaks form. Add 1/4C sugar and beat until the egg whites stiffen.

Spoon 1/3 of the egg whites into the chocolate mixture and fold until blended. Add the remaining egg whites and fold to blend completely.

Bake 45-55 minutes:
Pour the batter into 2 greased 9-inch spring form or cake pans. Bake at 325 degrees in the center of the oven.

Cool:
The cakes will fall when removed from the oven. Remove them from the oven and let them cool in their pans.

THE FROSTING

Melt:
Melt 4-6 oz. chocolate and 2-3T coffee in a double boiler. Cool to room temperature.

Mix:
Beat the whipping cream until it becomes stiff. Add the liqueur. Fold in the cooled chocolate mixture. Refrigerate until ready to use.

Layer and frost:
Place one cake on a serving platter. Frost the top. Place the second cake on the first. Frost the sides and top. Refrigerate until ready to serve.

Yields 1 Two Layer Cake

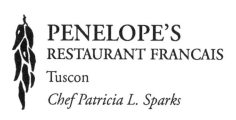

PENELOPE'S
RESTAURANT FRANCAIS
Tuscon
Chef Patricia L. Sparks

CHEESECAKE

1 Pound Cake, sliced thinly
3 pkgs. Cream Cheese, 8 oz. each
1/2 pint Sour Cream
4 Egg Yolks
3/4C Sugar
1t Vanilla
Juice and zest of 1/2 Lemon
2t Flour
4 Egg Whites
1/4C Sugar
Cherry Pie Filling or Fresh Fruit such as sliced
    kiwi or strawberries

Form crust:
Line a 10-inch spring form pan with pound cake slices. Press the
slices to the sides and bottom of the pan.

Blend:
Blend the cream cheese and sour cream at medium speed until
smooth. In another bowl, blend the egg yolks and 3/4C sugar. Blend
until the mixture turns pale yellow and smooth. Some sugar granules
can be present, but the mixture should not be coarse. Slowly add the
egg mixture to the cream cheese mixture. Mix until well blended.
Add the vanilla, lemon juice and zest, and flour. Blend well.

In a clean bowl, beat the egg whites at high speed until almost stiff.
Reduce the speed to slow-medium, and blend in 1/4C sugar.

Combine:
Pour 1/3 of the egg white mixture into the cream cheese mixture, and
fold well. Add the rest of the whites and fold until smooth. Pour the
filling into the crust.

Bake 1 hour:
Bake at 275 degrees.

Let sit 1 hour:
Turn off the oven, but do not open the door. Leave the cake in the oven for 1 hour.

Chill:
Chill until firm.

Topping:
Top with cherry pie filling or fresh fruit such as sliced kiwi or strawberries.

Refrigerate.

Yields 1 Cake

MICHAEL'S
FINE DINING
Page
Chef Michael J. Decker

PUMPKIN CHEESECAKE

14 oz. Almonds, finely ground
1/2C and 2T Sugar
8T Butter, melted
1-1/2 lbs. Cream Cheese
1-1/4C Sugar
1-1/2t Cinnamon
3/4t Ginger
Pinch of Cloves
2-1/4C Pumpkin
1/4C Heavy Cream
5 Eggs

Garnish:
Roasted Pumpkin Seeds

Mix:
Combine the almonds, 1/2C and 2T sugar, and butter.

Bake 5 minutes:
Press the mixture into a buttered 10-inch springform pan. Bake at 425 degrees until lightly toasted. Let cool.

Mix:
Soften the cream cheese in a mixer. Add 1-1/4C sugar, cinnamon, ginger, cloves, pumpkin, heavy cream, and eggs. Add the ingredients in the order listed. Mix well, but do not overbeat.

Bake 1 hour:
Pour the filling into the crust. Bake at 350 degrees. The cheesecake should be set when done.

Garnish and chill:
Garnish with roasted pumpkin seeds.
Serve chilled.

Yields 1 Cake

THE BOULDERS RESORT
LATILLA RESTAURANT
Carefree
Chef Brent E. Wertz

CRANBERRY NAUTICAL

5 cans whole jelled Cranberries, 12 oz. each
2-1/2 lbs. Cream cheese
6T Sour Cream
Sugar to taste
1/4C Walnuts

Whip:
Whip the cream cheese, sour cream and sugar.

Freeze:
Place the cranberries on the bottom of a baking pan. Spread the cheese mixture on top. Freeze.

Serve:
Remove the pan from the freezer, and dip it in hot water for 10 seconds. The nautical sides will melt, making removal easier. Flip the pan upside down so the nautical falls onto a serving plate. The cranberry layer will be on top. If desired, flip the nautical again so the cream cheese is on top. Sprinkle with walnuts.

Serves 12

NAUTICAL INN
Lake Havasu City
Chef Elaine Perritt

SOUFFLÉ GRAND MARNIER

1/2C Butter, melted
2/3C Flour
1-3/8C Milk
1/2t Lemon Rind, grated
1T Orange Rind, grated
Pinch of Salt
1/2C Grand Marnier
10 Egg Yolks
10 Egg Whites
3/4C and 1T Sugar

Mix:
Mix the butter and flour in a bowl.

Heat few minutes:
Bring the milk to a boil in a saucepan. Mix in the lemon rind, orange rind, and salt. Mix in the flour mixture. Cool 1 minute. Add the Grand Marnier. Slowly whisk in the egg yolks and cook on low heat until well blended.

Beat:
In a clean, dry bowl, begin beating the egg whites. As they become stiff, add the sugar and continue beating until firm peaks form. Do not overbeat.

Bake 20 minutes:
Brush a soufflé dish lightly with butter and dust with sugar. Very gently fold the egg whites into the egg yolk mixture. Fill the soufflé dish 3/4 full and bake at 375 degrees.

Cool:
When the soufflé is warm, it is very fragile. A slight bump can cause it to collapse. When done, turn the heat off and let the soufflé cool in the oven. Once it is cool, you should be able to move it freely without risking collapse.

Serves 10 to 12

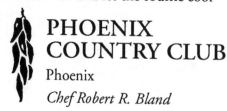

**PHOENIX
COUNTRY CLUB**
Phoenix
Chef Robert R. Bland

FLOURLESS CHOCOLATE SOUFFLÉ CAKE

9 oz. Chocolate
4-1/2 oz. Butter
6 Egg Yolks
6T Sugar
7 Egg Whites
2T Sugar
Powdered Sugar

Freeze:
Butter a 9-inch cake pan. Freeze. Dust with flour, and freeze again.

Melt and mix:
Melt the chocolate and butter in a double boiler. In a bowl, whip the egg yolks and 6T sugar until they reach ribbon consistency. In another bowl, whip the egg whites and 2T sugar until stiff peaks form. Fold the chocolate into the yolks, and then into the whites.

Bake 45 minutes:
Pour the mixture into the prepared cake pan. Bake at 425 degrees for 5 minutes, then at 325 degrees for 40 minutes.

Serve:
When the cake is cool, remove it from the pan, and dust with powdered sugar.

Yields 1 Cake

CHRISTOPHER'S
Phoenix
Chef Christopher Gross

NOUGAT GLACIERS

18 oz. Whipping Cream
3/4C Almonds, diced
1/4C Pistachios
1-1/4C Sugar
3 Egg Whites
1/2C Sugar

Garnish:
Fresh Berries
Mint

Prepare cream:
Whip the cream until stiff peaks form. Refrigerate.

Prepare nougat:
Spread the almonds and pistachios over a cookie sheet greased with salad oil.

Heat 1-1/4C sugar with just enough water to dissolve the sugar in a heavy pan over very low heat. Stir constantly until the sugar caramelizes.

Pour the caramelized sugar over the nuts and stir with a wooden spoon until it forms a stiff nougat. Turn the nougat onto a cutting board and chop it into small pieces. Sift the nougat and discard the sifted powder.

Prepare meringue:
In a bowl, whip the egg whites until stiff peaks form.

In a small saucepan, boil 1/2C sugar with just enough water to dissolve the sugar. Boil until the sugar turns clear.

Pour the hot syrup into the egg whites in a steady thin stream, whipping continuously. Continue whipping until the bowl has cooled.

Assemble glacier:
Fold the whipped cream, nougat, and meringue together. Be careful not to overfold, or the cream will break down.

Spray a terrine with nonstick spray, and cover the bottom with some of the nougat mixture. Tap the terrine sharply on your countertop to release any large air bubbles. Add more mixture and repeat until the terrine is full.

Freeze 24 hours.

Remove glacier from terrine and refreeze:
Soak the terrine in a sink of hot water until the sides release. Take the glacier out of the terrine, and place the glacier back in the freezer until its sides refreeze.

Serve:
Slice the glacier with a serrated knife and serve with fresh berry and mint garnish.

Serves 6

CHRISTOPHER'S
Phoenix
Chef Christopher Gross

PARNASSIENNE DE MOUSSE AU CHOCOLAT
Chocolate Tower

5-1/2 oz. Dark Chocolate
3T Unsalted Butter
1/4C Whipping Cream, whipped stiff
5 oz. Dark Chocolate
10 Egg Whites, whipped until stiff peaks form
Vanilla Sauce, recipe follows

Garnish:
2 pts. Raspberries or Blueberries
8 sprigs Mint

Melt and mix:
Place 5-1/2 oz. chocolate and butter in a medium bowl. Set the bowl in a water bath on top of the stove and let the water just simmer. Heat until melted, stirring occasionally with a wooden spoon. This should take about 5 minutes. At the same time, with a hand held mixer or whip, in a medium bowl, beat the heavy cream until stiff. Set aside. To finish the mousse, fold the chocolate and egg whites together, then fold the cream in with a spatula.

Form towers:
You will need 1 large sheet of parchment paper, tape, and a pastry bag. Cut the parchment paper in strips 3-1/2 inches high and 5 inches long. Cut 16 strips. Roll 8 strips into the shape of a tube and tape. Stand them up and fill them with mousse using a pastry bag.

Freeze:
Place the towers in the freezer until completely frozen.

Wrap the towers in chocolate:
Melt the remaining 5 oz. chocolate in a water bath. Coat one side of each of the remaining 8 parchment strips with the melted chocolate. Unwrap the frozen mousse. Wrap the coated parchment around the

mousse (chocolate side against the mousse) and refrigerate 5 minutes. Peel the paper off. The chocolate will remain around the mousse.

Serve:
Ladle Vanilla Sauce onto 8 plates, making sure to cover the entire bottom. Puree one pint of raspberries and put into a small-holed pastry bag. Draw straight lines, or spirals in the Vanilla Sauce. With the point of a knife, cut through the sauce and raspberry puree to form the designs. Place the chocolate mousse tower in the center of the plate and garnish the top with raspberries and mint sprig. Allow to defrost.

Yields 8 Towers

VANILLA SAUCE

> 8 Egg Yolks
> 3-1/2C Sugar
> 2C Half and Half
> 1/2T Vanilla Extract or 1/2 Vanilla Bean

Mix and heat:
With a hand-held mixer, cream the yolks and sugar in a medium bowl. At the same time, bring the Half and Half with the vanilla to a simmer in a medium sauce pot.

When the Half and Half is hot, temper the egg yolk and sugar mixture by adding 1/4C hot Half and Half. Stir well. Pour the egg and sugar mixture into the rest of the Half and Half and cook gently over low heat, stirring constantly. When the sauce is thick enough to coat the back of a spoon, strain and let cool.

CHRISTOPHER'S
Phoenix
Chef Christopher Gross

SPRING IN THE DESERT

Winner of the 1990 Scottsdale Culinary Festival Dessert
Competition, Spring in the Desert makes a very pretty presentation.

Roulade:
3 Eggs
3/4C Cake Flour
3/4C Sugar
1t Vanilla extract
1/4C clarified Butter
1 pinch Salt
Raspberry Marmalade

Turron:
1/2C Orange Juice
3 Egg Yolks
1/4C Sugar
2 Gelatin leaves, soaked in cold water until soft
13 oz. Whipped Cream

Ganache:
1/2C Cream
8 oz. Chocolate, grated
1/4C Honey

Gel:
1/2C Orange Juice
1/2C Sugar
1T Gelatin Powder

Use a wooden spoon throughout the recipe.

Prepare the roulade:
Whip the eggs, flour, and sugar until light. Fold in the vanilla,
butter, and salt by hand. Spread the batter 1/2 inch deep, evenly, on
a well greased cookie sheet.

Bake 10 minutes at 400 degrees until light brown. Cool and remove from pan.

Spread raspberry marmalade evenly over the roulade. Cut the cake into 1/8-inch slices and stack.

Freeze overnight.

Arrange the roulade in molds:
Slice the roulade into thin, even slices. Line the perimeter of 24 ring molds with roulade slices.

Prepare the orange turron:
Heat the orange juice in a saucepan over a medium flame until hot. Do not boil. Add the egg yolks and cook for about 10 minutes until the mixture sticks to your spoon. Do not allow lumps to form. Mix in the gelatin leaves. Cool. Fold in the whipped cream. Pipe turron inside the roulade.

Prepare the ganache:
Heat the cream over low heat. Add the chocolate and stir until melted. Add the honey. Cool. Pipe a ganache border around the top of each turron.

Prepare the orange gel:
Heat the orange juice, sugar, and gelatin powder until the gelatin dissolves. Cool. Pour the gel inside the ganache border.

Serve:
Remove the dessert from the molds. Serve two per person.

Serves 12

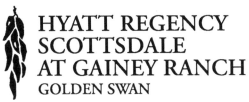

HYATT REGENCY
SCOTTSDALE
AT GAINEY RANCH
GOLDEN SWAN
Scottsdale
Chef Anton Brunbauer

CASSIS MOUSSE WRAPPED IN WHITE CHOCOLATE WITH HAZELNUT AND CHOCOLATE SAUCES

An elegant presentation of a black currant mousse combined with chocolate and hazelnut sauces. Raspberries on top are a lovely option.

2C Sugar
1/4C Water
8 Egg Yolks
1 qt. Cassis Puree
1C Creme de Cassis
1 qt. Whipping Cream, whipped to a soft peak
2C White Chocolate
Hazelnut Custard Sauce, recipe follows
Chocolate Sauce, recipe follows

Garnish:
Raspberries
Chocolate Curls

THE MOUSSE

Heat 10 minutes:
Place the sugar and 1/4C water in a saucepan large enough to hold 3 times the volume. Stir to mix before cooking. Do not stir once cooking has begun or crystals will form. Heat over a hot flame. At first, boiling will be easy and rapid, but it will slow as the syrup thickens. If you have a candy thermometer, cook until the mixture becomes thick and reaches the hard ball stage (250 to 260 degrees). If you don't have a thermometer, test by gently spooning some syrup out, and dropping it into ice water. When it has reached the hard ball stage, it will form a firm, sticky ball that does not crush easily. If the sugar separates into hard threads, you have cooked it too long.

Mix:
In a bowl, whip the egg yolks at high speed. Add the hot sugar mixture to the eggs in a thin steady stream. Whip until cool. Whip in the cassis puree and creme de cassis. Fold in the whipped cream.

Spoon into molds:
Spray 12 individual ring molds (cupcake sized) or 2 medium sized molds (6C each) with nonstick spray. Spoon the mousse into the molds. It will be easier to remove the mousse later if you use ring molds (without bottoms), but molds with bottoms will work.

Freeze, then remove from molds:
To remove mousse from a mold that has a bottom, set the mold in hot water for 10 seconds to thaw the sides. Then turn it upside down; the mousse will fall out. To remove the mousse from a ring mold, run a knife along the inside surface of the mold.

WRAP THE MOUSSE IN WHITE CHOCOLATE

Cut parchment paper:
Cut paper strips approximately 1/2 inch wider than the molds are high, and 1/4 inch longer than the mold circumference. Although you will not put the strips in the molds, the strips must be large enough to wrap around the molded mousse.

Melt and temper:
Melt the white chocolate in a double boiler (110 to 120 degrees). Place the melted chocolate in a bowl or on a marble slab, and work it with a spatula until it starts to thicken and becomes slightly pasty. Place the chocolate in the double boiler again and warm gently until it reaches spreading consistency.

Cool:
Spread the warm chocolate on the paper and allow it to set.

Wrap the mousse with chocolate:
Set the cooled chocolate on a baking sheet in a warm oven for a few seconds. Warm slightly until pliable, but not too soft. Wrap the chocolate around the mousse, leaving the paper on the outside.

Freeze.

(continued on next page)

Serve:

Remove the paper from the wrapped mousse. Serve on chilled plates with Hazelnut Custard Sauce and Chocolate Sauce on the side. Filling the top with raspberries or chocolate curls adds a nice touch.

Serves 12

HAZELNUT CUSTARD SAUCE

2C Milk
1 Vanilla Bean
1/2C Sugar
6 Egg Yolks
1/2C Praline Paste*

*Praline paste is available in gourmet stores, but may be hard to find. As a substitute, mix 2C hazelnuts, toasted and ground to the consistency of peanut butter, with 1/4C sugar.

Boil and cool:

Place the milk and vanilla bean in a saucepan. Bring to a boil. Allow to cool 10 minutes. When cooled, remove the vanilla bean.

Mix:

In a bowl, whip the sugar and yolks until they become thick and pale yellow. Add the milk and blend a little at a time.

Heat:

Gently heat the sauce at 180 degrees, stirring constantly until thick. Do not boil, or the egg yolks will curdle. Mix in the praline paste. Strain to remove any lumps that may have formed if the sauce cooked too long.

Chill.

CHOCOLATE SAUCE

1C Half and Half
2C Semi-sweet Chocolate, chopped
More cream or Frangelico, if needed

Boil and cool:
Bring the half and half to a boil in a saucepan. Pour the heated cream in a bowl, and add the chocolate. Allow to cool.

Whip:
Whip the sauce. Add more cream or a liqueur, such as Frangelico, as needed to thin. The final consistency should be just thick enough to coat the back of a spoon.

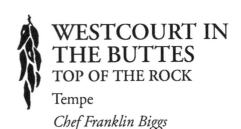

WESTCOURT IN
THE BUTTES
TOP OF THE ROCK
Tempe
Chef Franklin Biggs

CORNBREAD PUDDING WITH SWEET NUTMEG CREAM

3C Heavy Cream
1/3C Cornmeal
1C Milk, cold
2 Eggs
1/2C Molasses
1/2C Sugar
1/2t Cinnamon
1T fresh Ginger, finely chopped
1/2t Salt
4 oz. Unsalted Butter
Sweet Nutmeg Cream, recipe follows

Warm 25 minutes:
Warm the cream at very low heat in a saucepan or double boiler. Combine the cornmeal and milk in a bowl. Gradually add the cornmeal mixture to the cream, stirring constantly. Heat for 20 minutes.

Blend and add:
Place the eggs, molasses, sugar, cinnamon, ginger and salt in a food processor. Blend until smooth. Stir the puree into the cream mixture. Add butter and stir.

Bake 30 minutes:
Bake at 325 degrees in glass cookware until firm.

Serve:
Serve warm with Sweet Nutmeg Cream.

Serves 4

SWEET NUTMEG CREAM

1 pint Whipping Cream, whipped
1/2C Sugar
1t Nutmeg
1t Vanilla

Fold.

LOS ABRIGADOS
CANYON ROSE
Sedona
Chef Todd Hall

STRAWBERRIES DANIEL WITH DESSERT CREPES

DESSERT CREPES

1-1/2C Flour, all purpose
1-1/2C Milk
2t Vanilla extract
3 Eggs
1/4C Water
1/4C Sugar
1/4C Clarified Butter, slightly cooled
Sprinkling of Powdered Sugar

Mix:

Place the flour, milk, vanilla, eggs, water, and sugar in a 1 quart mixing bowl. Mix well. Add the butter and mix for 1 minute.

Chill 1 hour.

Fry 1 minute each:

Set the burner on medium-low heat. With a one ounce ladle, pour the batter evenly into a 7-inch nonstick saute pan, covering the pan bottom completely. Cook until the crepes leave the pan when shaken, about 30 seconds. Turn or flip the crepes and cook for 30 seconds on the other side. The first few crepes may not come out as well as those that follow, so don't get discouraged. Extra crepes can be stored in the freezer.

Deep fry 2 minutes each:

Float the pan fried crepe in sizzling hot vegetable oil, 4 inches deep. Place a metal bowl, metal muffin cup, or metal sieve (maximum 3-inch diameter) on top of the crepe. Let the bowl sink 3 inches. The crepe will rise and wrap around the sides of the bowl. As it cooks, it will assume the bowl's shape. Fry the crepe until golden brown and crisp.

Cool.

Top:

Sprinkle with powdered sugar.

Yields 15 crepes

STRAWBERRIES DANIEL

1 pint Strawberries or other fresh berries
2C Whipping Cream
2t Grand Marnier, optional
4 Dessert Crepes
4 scoops French Vanilla Ice Cream
4T Sweet Butter
3T Apricot Preserves
3T Marie Brizard Apricot Liqueur
4T Grand Marnier

Whip:
Whip the cream and 2t Grand Marnier.

Garnish the crepes:
Wash the strawberries and slice them in half. 16 strawberry halves will be used in the garnish; the rest will be mixed into the sauce.

Spread the whipped cream on 4 serving dishes. Lay a crepe on top of each, and place a scoop of ice cream on each crepe. Garnish with strawberry halves.

Heat several minutes:
Melt the butter and apricot preserves in a saute pan for a moment over low heat. Mix and cook until the butter melts. Add the liqueur and stir well. Add the reserved strawberries and mix. Sprinkle with cinnamon and stir well.

Flame:
Add 4T Grand Marnier to the sauce and ignite. Stir until the flames subside, and pour over the garnished crepes.

Serves 4

THE TACK ROOM
Tucson
The Kane and Vactor Family

CREPE SUZETTE

For a dramatic dessert, flame Crepe Suzette at the table.

Peels and juice of 2 Oranges
Peel of 1/2 Lemon
2T Sugar
6 oz. soft Butter
2T Grand Marnier
2T Cointreau
3 Eggs
1/4t Salt
1T Sugar
Few drops of Vanilla
1-1/2C Milk
1C Flour
6T Butter, melted

SUZETTE BUTTER

Peel:
With a vegetable peeler, lightly remove the outer pigmented layer of the orange and lemon peels, avoiding the white inner part. Remove only one side of the lemon. Save the peels and oranges for the next step.

Blend:
Blend the reserved peels and juice from both oranges until the peels are chopped. Add 2T sugar, butter, Grand Marnier and Cointreau. Blend well.

CREPES

Blend:
Blend eggs, salt, 1T sugar and vanilla at low speed for a few seconds. One at a time, slowly add and blend the milk, flour and butter.

Fry:

Cook the crepes in an 8-inch buttered frying pan over medium heat. Butter the pan lightly each time. Pour in about 2T batter, then quickly rotate the pan to cover the bottom completely. Cook until brown, then carefully turn with a spatula or by hand and brown the other side. Cook one crepe at a time.

HEAT THE CREPES IN SUZETTE BUTTER

Heat:

Melt 1/2C suzette butter in a chafing dish or shallow skillet. Heat the crepes one at a time in the suzette butter, adding more butter as needed.

FLAME

Fold each crepe into quarters. Ring a pan with the crepes, laying them in the same direction. Spoon suzette butter over the crepes. Adding 2t Grand Marnier will make flaming easier. Ignite. Baste with suzette butter to continue flaming.

Serves 8

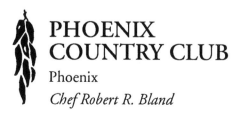

PHOENIX
COUNTRY CLUB
Phoenix
Chef Robert R. Bland

KOLACHIE

This recipe can be easily adjusted to make Swedish Butter Cookies, or Thumb Prints.

> 2C Pastry Flour
> 1C Powdered Sugar
> 1/4t Salt
> 1C Butter or Margarine
> 1T Vanilla
> Fruit Filling (apple, raspberry, lemon, apricot, etc.),
>   or Cream Cheese, or both!

Mix:
Combine the flour, sugar and salt in a bowl. Add the butter and use a fork or pastry blender to blend. Add the vanilla and blend.

Form kolachie:
Knead the above mixture until it forms a smooth dough. Roll the dough out until it is 1/4 inch thick. Cut circles, 4 inches in diameter. Spoon the fruit or cheese filling into the center of each circle. Fold the dough over the top, and pinch closed.

Bake 12 minutes:
Place the kolachie on a baking pan lined with parchment paper. Bake at 325 degrees until done but not brown.

Variations:
To make **Swedish Butter Cookies,** use this recipe, but do not use filling. Instead, add 1C chopped almonds to the dough, and roll it into balls. Bake at 325 degrees for 12 minutes.

To make **Thumb Prints,** press the centers of the dough circles with your thumb. Fill the wells with fruit filling, and bake the same as above.

Yields 3-4 dozen

SWISS VILLAGE BAKERY
Payson
Chef Diana Mitchell

TORTONI

3 Egg Yolks
1C Powdered Sugar
1/4C Rum
3/4C Almond Cookie Crumbs
1-1/2C Cream, whipped until thick
3 Egg Whites, beaten until stiff but not dry
3/4C Almond Cookie Crumbs

Mix:
Beat the egg yolks. Add powdered sugar and beat well. Add the rum
and 3/4C cookie crumbs and mix. Gently fold in the whipped
cream. Gently fold in the beaten egg whites.

Freeze:
Pour the batter into unbuttered custard cups and sprinkle with 3/4C
cookie crumbs. Freeze.

Serves 8

SCORDATO'S
RESTAURANT
Tucson
Chef Jim Scordato

CHOCOLATE MINT ICE CREAM

10 Egg Yolks
1-1/3C Sugar
1 qt. Milk
1/2C Cream
1C Cocoa
4 oz. Chocolate, semi-sweet
1C fresh Mint, coarsely chopped and loosely packed

Simmer several minutes:
Combine the egg yolks and sugar in a bowl. Pour the milk and
cream in a pot and bring to a boil. Gradually add the warm milk
and cream to the yolk mixture. Return the mixture to the pot.
Cook until thickened, stirring constantly.

Add and steep:
Remove the mixture from the heat, and while still warm, add the
cocoa, chocolate, and mint. Let it steep until the mint flavor is
strong. Then strain.

Freeze in ice cream machine:
Pour the mixture into an ice cream machine and freeze according to
the manufacturer's instructions.

Serves 8

CHRISTOPHER'S
Phoenix
Chef Christopher Gross

PRICKLY PEAR SORBET

3C Prickly Pear Juice
1/2C Lime Juice
1/2C Sugar

Mix all the ingredients. Pour the sorbet into an ice cream freezer and freeze according to the manufacturer's directions.

Yields 1 Quart

JANOS
Tucson
Chef Janos Wilder

RESTAURANT & CHEF BACKGROUND & INDEX

ALDO BALDO
Scottsdale
Chef Joseph DeLucia, pp. 36, 37, 48, 51, 53, 181, 200, 225

There are still surprises in cooking simple food. Chef Joseph DeLucia has a knack for finding exotic, playful alternatives to traditional Italian recipes. The result is a light, healthy, full flavored cuisine. Mr. DeLucia worked for several years under the direction of Steven Lombardi at Steamer's Genuine Seafood in Phoenix.

ARIZONA BILTMORE RESORT
ORANGERIE
Phoenix
Chef Peter Hoefler, pp. 168

Serving international guests since 1929, the Arizona Biltmore is considered Arizona's Grande Dame of resorts, and one of the best in the world. The four star, four diamond Orangerie owes its reputation in part to Executive Chef Peter Hoefler. A native of Germany, Mr. Hoefler brings his experiences from Hong Kong, Bermuda, Canada, and the renowned Plaza Hotel in New York. He is known for innovative presentations of classic European dishes.

ARIZONA CLUB
Scottsdale, Phoenix
Chef Scott Tompkins, pp. 162, 190

Serving pioneers before Arizona was a state, the 100 year old Arizona Club is the oldest in the southwest. It was established during the west's wilder days as one of a few genteel locations for socializing. The Phoenix club has kept its 1890 ambiance; many of the original furnishings and fixtures decorate the club.

Executive Chef Scott Tompkins developed his skills while growing up in Arizona and travelling extensively in Hong Kong and China. He prepares traditional Southwestern and far eastern meals with elegance.

AVANTI
Scottsdale, Phoenix
Chefs Angelo Livi and Raul Peña, pp. 107, 223

Owner Angelo Livi learned his craft in some of the finest restaurants in France, Germany, Switzerland, Spain, and a cruise ship that travelled the world. He used his insights to make Avanti one of the best in America. Avanti is on the National Registry for America's finest restaurants. It won Arizona Trend Magazine's Best Restaurant Award (2 years) and Golden Spoon Award (5 years), was named Best Expensive Italian Restaurant by New Times (5 years), and Best Continental Restaurant by Phoenix Magazine.

Chef Raul Peña, a native of Mexico, has cooked for restaurants throughout Italy, and is listed as one of America's Outstanding Chefs.

BIG MAN'S CATERING
Kingman
Chef Watkin Sells, pp. 157, 164, 177, 196, 210

Big Man's Catering is owned by Chef Watkin Sells. He specializes in creole seafood cuisine.

THE BOULDERS RESORT
LATILLA RESTAURANT
Carefree
Chef Brent E. Wertz, pp. 28, 44, 59, 61, 64, 78, 232, 242

Lifestyles of the Rich and Famous has named The Boulders Resort one of the top four resorts in the world. The Robb Report lists the resort as one of the world's top three, and Andrew Harper Hideaway Report has listed The Boulders as the best resort in the United States. Located in the high Sonoran desert, the five diamond resort takes its name from spectacular boulders that surround it. The restaurant is made of native wood and stone, with tremendous Ponderosa Pine trunks supporting a latilla ceiling.

Executive Sous Chef de Cuisine Brent Wertz serves meals inspired by traditional American cooking - Shaker, Amish, Cajun, Southern, and New England. He graduated with high honors from the Culinary Institute of America, and has cooked for the world renowned Arizona Biltmore. His meals have helped earn Latilla Restaurant a number seven in the world ranking by Conde Nast Readers' Choice.

CAFE TERRA COTTA
Tucson
Chef Donna Nordin, pp. 42

Executive Chef Donna Nordin has helped put Cafe Terra Cotta on the cutting edge of American cuisine. She is featured in the PBS series "Great Chefs of the West" and its companion cookbook, Southwest Taste. Ms. Nordin has been teaching in San Francisco and other locations since 1973. Cafe Terra Cotta is listed as one of the top restaurants in the country by Conde Nast, Best Southwestern Restaurant by Tucson Weekly and Tucson Lifestyle, and has been featured in Gourmet and Bon Appetit magazines.

CHEZ RENE'S SWISS CHALET
Wickenburg
Chef Rene Lenggenhager, pp. 87, 180, 189

Rene Lenggenhager was born in Switzerland and attended the culinary school in Montreaux. On vacation in America 10 years ago, Mr. Lenggenhager stopped in Wickenburg to inspect some land for a friend. Taken by the plentiful horseback riding, sunshine, and friendly atmosphere, he returned to make Wickenburg home. Chez Rene's is now a popular spot for locals and visitors. Mr. Lenggenhager and his wife Inge, serve Swiss, French, Italian, and Western American cuisine.

CHOPANDAZ AFGHANI CUISINE
Tempe
Chef Shuja Ahmad, pp. 62, 136

Owner Shuja Ahmad offers authentic dishes from his homeland, Afghanistan. They have earned Chopandaz the Phoenix New Times 'Best Afghani Food' distinction for the past three years, Travel Holiday's Good Value Dining Award, and the adoration of Elin Jeffords, Food Critic for the Arizona Republic.

CHRISTOPHER'S
Phoenix
Chef Christopher Gross, pp. 216, 235, 245, 246, 248, 264

Christopher Gross opened Christopher's in 1990 with wildly imaginative contemporary French and American cuisine. During its first year, Christopher's was recognized as Best New Restaurant by USA Today and Esquire Magazine, and Best New Restaurant, Best French Restaurant, and Best Place to Blow Big Bucks by New Times.

Mr. Gross began his extraordinary career in Phoenix at age 14, and honed his skills in some of the finest restaurants of Europe and the United States. He was named one of America's Ten Best Chefs by Food and Wine Magazine, was one of 12 U.S. Chefs to compete in the Bocuse D'or Competition in Chicago, and is co-founder of Toque Blanche, an international chef's association.

COTTAGE PLACE
Flagstaff
Chef Kurt Gottschalk, pp. 41, 109

Executive Chef Kurt Gottschalk was raised in Holland,where he apprenticed at the Hotel Princess Juliana, Holland's finest. After working at exquisite restaurants throughout Holland and the United States, he and his wife, Sharley, opened Cottage Place.The restaurant is a melange of old and new- blending 1920's nostalgia and traditional Continental cuisine with innovative menu items and art. The Gottschalks are members of the Chaine des Rotisseurs and the American Culinary Federation (ACF).

DANIEL'S
Tucson
Chef Daniel Scordato, pp. 38, 60, 122

Bon Appetit has declared Daniel's the Best Northern Italian Restaurant in Arizona. Tucson Lifestyle readers voted Daniel's the Best Restaurant in Tucson for each of its five years. Owner Daniel Scordato serves new and traditional Italian cuisine. He learned his art from generations of family cooks, as well as one of Italy's most prominent chefs, Giuliano Bugialli. For the past three years, Mr. Scordato has won the Veuve Coicquot gold medal for matching food with spirits.

DEJA VU
Lake Havasu City
Chef Carl Husbands, pp. 178, 234

European influence is alive in Lake Havasu City, where the London Bridge spans

Lake Havasu waters, and Deja Vu cooks up nouveau French cuisine. Chef Carl Husbands uses his 20 years experience, the restaurant's herb garden, and food fresh from neighboring fields to create his original dishes.

EL CHARRO
Tucson
Chef Carlotta Flores, pp. 98

El Charro was established in 1922 by Tucson's First Businesswoman, Monica Flynn, with the mottos "La hambre hace salir el lobo de la cueva" (hunger makes the wolf leave his cave), and "Mi casa es su casa". Ms. Flynn always had food for anyone who needed it, whether or not they could pay. El Charro is currently run by Carlotta Flores, Monica's grandniece. It is housed in Carlotta's old home, now a National Historic Landmark Home. Monica's father built it of stones from Tucson's "A" Mountain.

The recipes used at the restaurant are those Monica started with. Some are featured in their book, El Charro and its Colorful Past. El Charro has also been presented in Gourmet Magazine, USA Today, the Opreyland USA television show, and a scene from Fr. Andrew Greeley's novel, Rite of Spring.

EL TOVAR
Grand Canyon
Chef Esteban Colon, pp. 18, 118, 125

Overlooking one of the wonders of the world, El Tovar Lodge is considered one of the great hotels of its time. Built in 1905, water was originally hauled in from 120 miles away. Today, the log and boulder lodge provides rustic, comfortable shelter, and fine regional cuisine.

Executive Chef Esteban Colon is a tribute to what can happen when one puts his heart and soul into every day. One of 18 children, Esteban left his Puerto Rican home at age 16. He and his sister moved to America, speaking no English. Their first home in the 'land of opportunity' was Harlem. Mr. Colon washed dishes without pay in order to learn from some of New York's finest culinary experts. He is now honored as one of America's Outstanding Chefs. Mr. Colon has been at the Grand Canyon for 10 years, adding a touch of Puerto Rican tradition to his Southwestern dishes.

ENCHANTMENT RESORT
Sedona
Chef Gerald Peters, pp. 83, 94, 144

A 180 degree view of Sedona's Red Rock cliffs is one of the pleasures of the world class, 4 star, 4 diamond Enchantment Resort. Executive Chef Gerald Peters helps earn these distinctions with his authentic Southwestern dishes and light, healthy cooking. Mr. Peters' honors include first prizes for Mexican cuisine, classical buffet, original pastries, and contributions to the culinary profession.

GREEKFEST
Phoenix, 2 locations
Chef Tony Makridis, pp. 220, 228

Greekfest has been satisfying local and international guests for 11 years. Their special style of traditional Aegean cooking is based on Owner Tony Markidis' family recipes. They came to America from Chios, Greece. Among its laurels, Greekfest has earned The New Times "Best Greek Restaurant" award every year since 1984.

The new Greekfest offers a taste of Hellenic spirit and lifestyle. Built in classical Byzantine and Greek island architecture, the restaurant features a folk museum of art, music, and publications.

HASSAYAMPA INN
Prescott
Chef Linda Rose, pp. 14, 138

Hassayampa Inn is Prescott's grand hotel. Hosting guests since 1927, it is listed on the National Register of Historic Places. Much of the original decor still graces the Inn. Chef Linda Rose prepares fine French and Northern Italian cuisine. She is a graduate of the Culinary Institute of America, and previously operated a restaurant in Tompkins Cove, New York.

HAVANA CAFE
Phoenix
The Hernandez Family, pp. 100, 146

Betty Jane and Gilbert Hernandez opened Havana Cafe in 1989, serving family recipes Gilbert brought with him when he left Cuba 40 years ago. After its first year, the cafe was chosen as Phoenix's Best Cuban Restaurant by New Times, and was awarded Holiday Travel Magazine's award for excellence.

Gilbert began his career in electronics, but could not deny his love for the restaurant business. He switched to dishwashing to learn the ropes, and worked his way up to cooking for some of the finest valley restaurants, and running a catering business with Betty Jane. Betty Jane started out as an artist, and turned to follow her family's path in the food business.

HOUSE OF CHAN
Kingman
Chef Tommy Chan, pp. 148

Owner Tommy Chan began his career as a child in China, helping in his family's and neighbors' restaurants. His wife Mary, also from China, is the third generation of her family to own a restaurant in Kingman. For nearly 30 years the Chans have been offering premiere Chinese and American food, and a lovely view of the mountains. The House of Chan is a member of AAA.

HYATT REGENCY SCOTTSDALE AT GAINEY RANCH
GOLDEN SWAN
Scottsdale
Chef Anton Brunbauer, pp. 16, 76, 116, 250

Born into a family of Austrian restauranteurs and innkeepers, Anton Brunbauer's career began as an apprentice at age 15. Since then, he has worked in some of the finest hotels and restaurants in Austria, Switzerland, Germany, Lichtenstein, and the United States. Mr. Brunbauer helped establish the first Arizona chapter of Toques Blanches, an international culinary organization. His honors include medals in the Chefs Masters Competition for Pastry and Most Creative Use of Beef.
Hyatt Regency Scottsdale is listed as one of the outstanding resorts of the world. Golden Swan has won multiple medals in international culinary competitions. They serve contemporary American cuisine with a distinct Southwestern influence.

THE IMPECCABLE PIG
Scottsdale
Chef Shane Taggart, pp. 34, 55, 89, 188, 194

The Impeccable Pig feels like home to many of its established clientele. A warm ambiance is created by a collection of quilts and antiques, and by its personal atmosphere. Meals are prepared in the dining room where guests are welcome to talk with the chefs and explore the collections.

INN AT McCORMICK RANCH
PINON GRILL
Scottsdale
Chef Farn Boggie, pp. 112, 142

Executive Chef Farn Boggie hails from London, where he earned the distinction of being the youngest Third Chef in England. At 19, he was cooking for such notables as the Queen of England, Prince Phillip, and former Prime Minister Harold Wilson.
Pinon Grill is one of the valley's finest; it has been honored with Diversion Magazine's 'Best Southwest Cuisine as an Art' and Trend Magazine's 'Silver Plate' awards.

JANOS
Tucson
Chef Janos Wilder, pp. 13, 31, 74, 156, 265

Owner and Author Janos Wilder prepares a rare blend of French and Southwestern cuisine. His cooking has earned honors from the James Beard Foundation, and has enabled him to publish Janos Recipes - Tales from a Southwest Restaurant. The Four Star Janos is located in an adobe Historic Landmark Home, circa 1855.

JOHN JACOB'S EL PARADOR
Tucson
Chefs Daniel Jacob and Consuelo Flores, pp. 7, 82

When John Jacob's El Parador opened, there were only three Mexican restaurants in Tucson; now there are 107.Family owned since 1946, three of John Jacob's children, Loretta and twins Donald and Daniel, now help run El Parador. Chef Consuelo Flores, a native of Mexico, has been with the restaurant since 1948. The Jacobs and Ms. Flores cook with "corozon y ganas" (heart and desire). "It's how you put the ingredients together that makes the difference."

KEATON'S RESTAURANT, GRILL & BAR
Tucson
Chef Tom Firth, pp. 32, 54, 206

Keaton's has a reputation for fresh seafood and a full menu of well-prepared fare. They recently expanded to three new locations: Buddy's Grill in Tucson, and Buster's restaurant in Scottsdale and Flagstaff.

THE LANDMARK RESTAURANT
Mesa
Chef Eric Foust, pp. 106, 128

Constructed in 1908, the building that houses the Landmark Restaurant was originally a Mormon Church. Later, it became the first home for Mesa Community College. Now, the Victorian style Landmark is in its 10th year, and is one of a few urban restaurants where one can find old-fashioned American cooking. Chef Eric Foust attended the Culinary Institute of America in Hyde Park, New York and has been in the restaurant business 15 years.

LOEWS VENTANA CANYON RESORT
VENTANA ROOM
Tucson
Chefs Tim Fields, Brian Light, Takashi Shiramizu, pp. 50, 131, 170, 172, 176, 212

Loews Ventana Canyon Resort is set in the Catalina foothills. Having received numerous awards, including Arizona Trend's Golden Spoon Award, the Ventana Room has gained international acclaim. This recognition is due in part to the skills of Chefs Tim Fields, Brian Light and Takashi Shiramizu.

Executive Sous Chef Fields was raised in Tucson. His inspiration towards a culinary career came from Catalina High School's Feast Program. Since then Mr. Fields has studied Cajun, creole, and Southwest cooking with such well-known chefs as Jonathan Landeen.

Brian Light graduated from the Culinary Institute of America. Before coming to Loews, he cooked for El Coyote in White Rock, Canada.

Japan's Takashi Shiramizu began his career in his uncle's butcher shop in Nora. He moved to Italy at 24, then on to Switzerland, France, Canada, Normandy, and England's Restaurant Mirabelle at Buckingham Palace. Mr. Shiramizu's talents lie in the art of plate presentation and the rare combination of classic French and Oriental cuisines.

LOS ABRIGADOS RESORT
CANYON ROSE
Sedona
Chef Todd Hall, pp. 8, 39, 52, 70, 182, 256

Mr. Hall is Captain of the Arizona Culinary Team, and is considered one of the most distinguished chefs in America. His culinary honors include being a finalist for the Boucuse D'or American Culinary Gold Cup, and winner of the Arizona Seafood Challenge, and ACF Gold, Silver, and Bronze medals.

The four diamond Los Abrigados serves continental cuisine, wine from its award winning collection, and offers a "spontaneity dinner". At the dinner, each guest is served a different dish during each of six courses. The dishes are chosen by the chef (at his whim).

MACY'S EUROPEAN COFFEEHOUSE AND BAKERY
Flagstaff
Chef Sue-Bug Skelton, pp. 33, 84, 226

Chef Sue-Bug Skelton and her staff prepare healthy food, using only the finest organic ingredients. They take pride in creating vegetarian, dairy-free and wheat-free alternatives to traditional dishes. All highly creative individuals, the cooks work as a team to develop their original recipes. Ms. Skelton has been a home baker since she was a child.

THE MANSION CLUB
Phoenix
Chef Peter Inauen, pp. 126, 150, 208

The Mansion Club is located in William Wrigley's former winter cottage. Built in 1929, the Wrigleys vacationed there until 1972. The mansion was converted into an award winning private club in 1980, but closed in June, 1991 to await new ownership.

MARRIOTT MOUNTAIN SHADOWS
SHELLS
Scottsdale
Chef Christopher R. Klett, pp. 192, 202

Voted Best Seafood Restaurant by New Times, Shells offers a full menu of innovative seafoods. Chef Kristopher Klett graduated from the Indian Hills Culinary School in Ottumwa, Iowa and attended Marriott's chefs program.

MICHAEL'S FINE DINING
Page
Chef Michael J. Decker, pp. 68, 141, 207, 240

Michael's staff enjoys catering for weddings, film companies, and other romantic and festive events such as the surpise dinner one gentleman arranged for his wife. The dinner was catered on Antelope Island, complete with bartender and waitperson in black tie.

Owner Michael Decker began his career in engineering, but found his true calling in the culinary arts. He studied at the New Orleans culinary institute, and has operated restaurants in Eagle Nest and Angel Fire, New Mexico.

MOLLY BUTLER LODGE
Greer
Chef Stephen R. Cooksley, pp. 86, 88

The Molly Butler Lodge is housed in the oldest lodge in Arizona, circa 1880, where the Butler family sold their first meal in 1909 for 25 cents. Although the lodge changed hands in 1965, the Butler name and down home cooking have carried on.

NAUTICAL INN
Lake Havasu City
Chef Elaine Perritt, pp. 40, 243

Lake Havasu is one of Arizona's largest tourist attractions. Located on the waterfront, the Nautical Inn is surrounded by lush landscape. They serve American, German, and Italian fare.

NAVAJO CAFE
Navajo
Chef Sarah Spencer, pp. 97

The town of Navajo was established in 1863 as the first territorial capitol of Arizona. Opening around the turn of the century, Navajo Cafe was at first, only a stagecoach station where passengers dined. Later, trains would stop for meals three times a day. Chef Sarah Spencer has been cooking at the cafe for 27 years.

NAVAJO NATION INN
Window Rock
Chef Regis Tsosie, pp. 29, 121

Navajo Nation Inn sits on the largest Indian reservation in the United States, near the Painted Desert, Hubbell Trading Post National Monument, Window Rock National Monument, and Canyon de Chelly. The Inn is owned and operated by the Navajo Indian Tribe. Recipes included in this book are traditional Navajo.

OAK CREEK OWL
Sedona
Chef Sean Cooke, pp. 58, 71, 72

Dramatic red rocks surround Sedona's oldest restaurant, the Oak Creek Owl. Chef Sean Cooke has been honored as one of the Outstanding Chefs of Northern America, and is a member of the International Association of Culinary Professionals. "The mind and body are but channels," he says, "great food flows from the spirit." The Oak Creek Owl serves fine Continental cuisine.

PENELOPE'S RESTAURANT FRANÇAIS
Tucson
Chef Patricia L. Sparks, pp.11, 120, 238

Penelope's, an intimate restaurant, offers a rotating four-entree menu of 6 course French meals. Penelope's has been honored as Best French Restaurant by Tucson Magazine, and has won the Silver Spoon Award from Arizona Trend, Silver Medal from Tucson Lifestyles, and Best Pairing Dessert with Champagne from Veuve

Cliquot. Owner Patricia Sparks has been cooking for over 20 years. She began her career with a bachelor's degree in Foods and Nutrition, and several years experience in test kitchens.

THE PHOENICIAN
MARY ELAINE'S
Scottsdale
Chef Alessandro Stratta, pp. 67, 184, 204

Executive Chef Alessandro Stratta's Northern Italian family has been in the hotel and restaurant business for four generations spanning Europe, the Americas, and Far and Near East. Raised in Italy, France, Singapore, and Pakistan, Chef Stratta has gained a culinary expertise that far exceeds his 26 years of age. Since graduating with honors from the California Culinary Institute in San Francisco in 1984, Chef Stratta has developed his distinctive culinary style while working in Monte Carlo, Beverly Hills, San Francisco, and New York.

Mary Elaine's offers Mediterranean Country cuisine, world class wines, a valuable art collection, and inspiring views of the Valley of the Sun.

THE PHOENICIAN
THE TERRACE DINING ROOM
Scottsdale
Chef David Hough, pp. 20

Chef de Cuisine David Hough graduated from the Culinary Institute of America. His 15 years experience includes positions as Sous Chef at Seapines Executive Conference Center, Hilton Head, South Carolina, and Executive Sous Chef at the Hyatt Regency hotels in Bethesda and Sarasota. He prepares Italian American fare at the elegant Terrace Dining Room.

THE PHOENICIAN
WINDOWS ON THE GREEN
Scottsdale
Chef Lenard Rubin, pp. 6, 30, 80, 103

Chef de Cuisine Lenard Rubin studied at the exclusive School for American Chefs in Napa Valley, and has worked at top restaurants throughout the country. His extensive awards include first places for lamb and hot food at C. Orby Anderson Culinary Arts Salon competitions, and first places for seafood at the Ocean Garden Shrimp Cooking and Arizona Seafood Challenges. Mr. Rubin represented Arizona in the 1990 American Seafood Challenge.

Windows on the Green serves cuisine influenced primarily by Native American and Hispanic cultures, set to a background of live Spanish guitar music.

PHOENIX COUNTRY CLUB
Phoenix
Chef Robert R. Bland, pp. 12, 244, 260

Executive Chef Robert Bland's 32 year career has been full and rewarding. He has worked at The Mansion Club, the Arizona Biltmore, and Grand Teton National Park, and has earned bountiful honors. Among them are the Thurston Dupar

Inspirational Award, Phoenix Thunderbird Chef of the Year, ACF National Recognition and President's Awards, Arizona Chef of the Year, and two nominations for ACF Chef of the Year.

PINK PEPPER THAI CUISINE
Scottsdale, Mesa, Phoenix
Chef Tony Tavee, pp. 124, 152, 201

Mr. Tavee was born in Bangkok and began his career at age 12, helping his widowed mother in her open air restaurant. Mrs. Tavee, also a Thai native, managed two restaurants in Los Angeles, famous for their celebrity clientele. Having worked hard throughout their lives, Owners Tony and Annie Tavee believe diligence and initiative are the essence of success. The Pink Pepper has been named as Phoenix Magazine's Favorite Thai Restaurant. It has also been listed by New Times as having the 'Best Thai Food' (6 years), and 'Best Ambiance'.

THE PLAINSMAN
Holbrook
Chef Gary Inzano, pp. 10, 102

For Executive Chef Gary Inzano, one pleasure of cooking is meeting travellers from all over the world that come to see Petrified National Park. Mr. Inzano prepares American meals tableside for his guests. His distinctions include 1st prizes for Seafood Buffet and Breads from the National Restaurant Association, and graduation from the Culinary Institute of America.

RAFFAELE'S
Mesa, Phoenix
Chef Raffaele Contacessi, pp. 123, 139

Co-owners Raffaele Contacessi and Lauretta Melchiori are enjoying the opening of their second restaurant in three years. Chef Contacessi creates his exquisite, signature Northern and Southern Italian dishes with true pride and passion. Mr. Contacessi studied at the Institute Culinario di Poggaio Franco in Bari, Italy.

RANCHO DE LOS CABALLEROS
Wickenburg
Chef Daniel Martin, pp. 65, 96, 154

Rancho de los Caballeros has been operating as a guest ranch since 1947. In addition to a wide range of modern recreational activities, the 20,000 acre ranch offers hay rides, horseback riding lessons, and cookouts in the desert. Chef Daniel Martin prepares a full menu in keeping with the Southwestern atmosphere of the ranch.

RED LION'S LA POSADA RESORT
THE GARDEN TERRACE
Paradise Valley
Chefs Marie Gamalski and David Harbula, pp. 160, 218, 224, 236

Guests at The Garden Terrace have been treated to a picturesque view of Camelback Mountain for 20 years. Chefs Marie Gamalski and David Harbula offer an eclectic contemporary menu. Ms. Gamalski graduated from the Culinary Institute of

America. Among her distinctions are a unique talent for fashioning award winning bread dough sculptures. The intricate, creative qualities of pastry cooking enticed Pastry Chef David Harbula to pursue his specialty. Mr. Harbula has been creating desserts for seven years. He previously worked at The Registry and Upper Crust.

SCORDATO'S RESTAURANT
Tucson
Chef Jim Scordato, pp. 9, 93, 108, 233, 263

Nestled at the base of the Tucson Mountains, and serving authentic Italian cuisine, Scordato's is reminiscent of a desert Italian Villa. Established in 1972, the restaurant won Arizona Trend's prestigious Gold Spoon Award, has been voted as one of Tucson's Top Five Best Restaurants by Tucson Lifestyle readers, and has earned Mobil's three star rating for the past four years. Owner Jim Scordato learned to cook with generations of family chefs, including brother Daniel (Daniel's).

SHERATON TUCSON
EL CONQUISTADOR
Tucson
Chefs Alan Zeman and Christine Dettloff, pp. 22, 195, 198, 237

Executive Chef Alan Zeman graduated first in his class with high honors at the Culinary Institute of America and received the coveted Dean's Award for Professionalism, presented only 19 times in the school's history. Mr. Zeman is featured as one of the Great Chefs of the West in the PBS Great Chefs television series. He has written feature articles for Bon Appetit Magazine, chairs top culinary competitions, teaches cooking classes throughout Arizona, markets his own line of Southwestern seasonings (Chef Alan Zeman's Southwest Originals), and is President of the Chefs Association of Southern Arizona. Among his many other honors, Mr. Zeman was voted Chef of the Year by his colleagues in the chefs association.

Ms. Dettloff worked as Sous Chef and Pastry Chef at several of Tucson's finest restaurants, including the Painted Desert, Jerome's, and Janos. At Sheraton Tucson, she manages pastry production for banquets, the Country Club, and six restaurants. Her pastries have helped earn Tucson Lifestyle Magazine's Best Brunch in Tucson acclaim.

SOLARIUM RESTAURANT
Tucson
Chef Jonathan Landeen, pp. 46, 56, 155, 186

The Solarium was created by a group of artists as a statement in wood, glass, sun, life, and our relationship with nature. Blending with the desert landscape, the restaurant offers a magnificent view of the Catalinas.

Among Mr. Landeen's laurels are gold medals in hot food competitions, finalist at the American Seafood Challenge, and Chef of the Year (voted by his colleagues in the ACF Chefs Association of Southern Arizona).

SWISS VILLAGE BAKERY
Payson
Chef Diana Mitchell, pp. 26, 27, 262

Swiss chalets dot the village of Payson in Arizona's high country. One of the most prominent is the Swiss Village Bakery. Established in 1972, it has become a local landmark. Townspeople say "We're just 2 blocks south of the bakery." Ms. Mitchell is famous for her fresh pastries and baked goods.

THE TACK ROOM
Tucson
The Kane and Vactor Family, pp. 81, 92, 140, 153, 158, 258

The Tack Room recently became the third restaurant in history to receive its 15th consecutive five star rating. (12 restaurants in the country are currently rated 5 star). An AAA Four Diamond rating, Nation's Restaurant News Fine Dining Hall of Fame, and Who's Who in American Restaurants are just a few more of the Tack Room's steady stream of honors for its innovative Southwestern and American meals.

Several members of the Kane and Vactor family grew up in the hacienda that now houses the restaurant. The family has owned The Tack Room for 40 years. As is common with five star restaurants, it is now managed by the third generation. The family believes a successful restaurant matures over time with the continuous belief that "our reputation will be made tonight".

WESTCOURT IN THE BUTTES
TOP OF THE ROCK
Tempe
Chef Franklin Biggs, pp. 110, 166, 174, 252

Westcourt in the Buttes is set on a high butte overlooking the Valley of the Sun. The 4 diamond resort was chosen by Conde Naste Traveler Magazine readers as one of the top 100 hotels in the world. Its depth of quality is shown by honors ranging from Successful Meetings Magazine's Pinnacle Award to honors for environmental improvement and arid landscaping. Top of the Rock is named by Tempe Magazine as the Top Romantic Restaurant, Top Spot to Impress Out of Towners, and Top Expensive Dinner. New Times cites Top of the Rock as the spot for the Best Romantic Meal, and the restaurant has taken first place at the Mayor's Culinary Cup Dessert Competition for the past three years.

Mr. Biggs is a graduate of La Varenne in Paris. He cooked for Deer Valley Resort, Claremont Resort and Spa, and The Lodge at Pebble Beach. He prepares a menu of Southwestern dishes complemented with specialties from around the world.

• Currently, only 12 restaurants in the nation are rated as five star (Mobil rating).
• New Times is a Phoenix newspaper with an emphasis on entertainment.
• ACF stands for American Culinary Federation

TECHNIQUES AND TERMS

Alcohol, adding:
Use caution anytime you add alcohol to a hot, nearly dry pan; it may ignite. For more information, see "Flaming".

Beans, cooking dried:
Dried, unprepared beans need to be tenderized. Soak the beans overnight in room temperature water (3 times as much water as beans). Drain the water. Place the beans in a pot and cover with fresh water. Bring to a boil, reduce the heat, and simmer for 1 hour (garbanzos), 2 hours (black beans), or 2-1/2 to 3 hours (pintos). Keep an eye on the water to make sure the beans stay covered.

If you can't soak the beans overnight, soak them as long as possible, and increase simmering time. Or, bring the beans and water to a boil, simmer two minutes, and remove from heat. Cover the pot and let them stand for about an hour.

Brown gravy or sauce:
To make a quick brown sauce, when done cooking meat, remove it from the pan. While the drippings are still boiling hot, add flour (add an amount of flour equal to the dripping volume), and mix well with a fork. Add stock or water, stirring, until you reach your desired consistency. Simmer five to eight minutes over low heat on the stovetop or in the oven. The mixture will thicken as you heat it. Add more liquid as needed to return to desired consistency.

Deep fry:
If you are using batter, one gourmet trick is to let the batter rest for two hours before coating the food and cooking. A subtle difference, it keeps the batter lighter, less doughy.

To deep fry, immerse the food in very hot oil (350 degrees) for a few seconds to a few minutes until crispy. If the oil is cooler than 350 degrees, the food will absorb oil.

Deglaze:
Deglazing releases valuable flavors trapped in a pan after sauteeing. To deglaze, add water, stock, or wine to a very hot pan and swish.

Within a few seconds, flavors trapped in the pan will dissolve into the liquid, and become part of the sauce. Food is typically removed from the pan before deglazing, although some recipes allow food to remain.

Double boiler:
Double boiling ensures an even, gentle heat for foods that can be ruined by overheating. To make a double boiler, place water in a pot, and set a heat-safe bowl on top of the pot. The water should not touch the bottom of the bowl when boiling. Place the food to be heated in the bowl, and bring the water to a boil.

Filo or phyllo dough, working with:
Filo comes in paper thin sheets. It dries out and becomes brittle very quickly. The best technique is to organize ahead of time, and work quickly once you have opened the package. If you are interrupted, you can try laying a damp cloth over the filo, but this can make the dough too damp, and the cloth can stick to the dough.

Flaming:
Flaming burns off alcohol, but leaves a spirit's flavor behind. Heat the pan until it is very hot. Take the pan away from the stove and add the alcohol. On a gas stove, return the pan to the burner and tip slightly. The burner flame will ignite the sauce. On an electric stove, ignite with a long match. Place the match near the edge of the pan - if you reach towards the middle, you may scorch your arm. Stir continuously while flaming to ensure that any alcohol that has run to the bottom of the pan is exposed to air and can burn off.

As an alternative to flaming, reduce the alcohol by at least half (see "Reduce").

Peppers - roasting, peeling, and deseeding:
Roasting fresh green peppers enhances flavor. Peeling and deseeding is mainly for aesthetics, and in some cases, to remove bitterness or hot seeds. If you are in a hurry, you can prepare green peppers that have not been roasted or peeled. Canned chilies are already roasted, peeled and deseeded.

In the Southwest, many markets sell fresh roasted chilies at harvest time, September. A popular tradition is to buy the roasted chilies, and freeze them for use throughout the year. You can peel and deseed before or after freezing. Be sure to freeze only dry chilies; wet chilies turn to mush after thawing.

You can also roast your own fresh chilies. Several methods are described below. For each method, never touch your eyes or mouth while you have chile oil on your hands. The oil can burn sensitive tissues.

Direct Flame Method for Parching Skin
Pierce green chilies 2 or 3 times each with a fork. Hold them near a flame, or place them on your oven rack under a broiler. Heat and turn continuously until the chilies become puffy and brown (some prefer blackened). Immediately set the chilies in a covered container, and let them rest for 15-20 minutes.

Boiling Oil Method for Parching Skin
Pierce each green chile 2 or 3 times with a fork. Heat oil in a mini-fryer according to manufacturer's directions for french fries; or half fill a deep, heavy saucepan with oil, and heat until a thermometer reaches the deep frying mark or 350 degrees. Immerse 2 or 3 chilies at a time into the oil, and heat until blisters form. Immediately remove the chilies and submerge them in a bowl of cold water.

To Peel
After parching the skin, and when cool enough to handle, the skins will easily slip off. To make Chilies Rellenos more attractive (and to prove you are not using canned chilies), leave the stems intact.

For Wimps
Often the hottest parts of a chile are the seeds and the cord that runs inside the chili length. Scrape them out, and few people will know you cheated.

(Direct flame method and boiling oil methods for peeling chilies were contributed by Chef Carlotta Flores, El Charro)

Piping sack or pastry bag:
A piping sack is a tube used to squeeze contents (creamy filling) onto a cake or other surface, often in a decorative shape. The technique is called piping.

Red chile, making powder or sauce:
Most red chilies are green chilies that have turned red as they dry out. When dried, crush the red chilies to make powder, or blend with enough water to make a thin sauce. The sauce can be frozen and used as needed.

Reduce:
Reducing a liquid concentrates flavors, thickens the sauce, and/or burns off alcohol. To reduce, simmer until the desired volume or thickness is reached. To evaporate alcohol, reduce until the alcohol volume has decreased by half.

Remove frozen food from container:
It is possible to get frozen food from a container without gouging the sides. Set the container in hot water for 10 seconds to melt the contents from the sides. Flip the container upside down. The contents should fall out.

Ribbon consistency:
A batter has reached ribbon consistency when it runs off a spatula or spoon, forming an uninterrupted "ribbon" (thin flat stream) for a few seconds.

Roux:
Roux is used to thicken sauces. It can be made in large quantities and stored in the refrigerator for use in other recipes. To make roux, bring oil, fat, or butter to a boil. Add an equal amount of flour and whisk with a fork until smooth. Simmer on the stovetop or bake at 325 degrees for 5 to 8 minutes, stirring occasionally.

If you will be adding roux to a brown sauce, you may use a little extra heat to brown the roux slightly (stir continuously as you make the roux). When adding roux to any sauce, pour slowly and stir continuously. Use only as much roux as needed to thicken the sauce to desired consistency.

Sauce, straining:
Straining sauces is an optional fine cooking technique used to make them smoother.

Seafood - purchasing, curing, marinating, boiling:
Be sure to purchase only closed shellfish. They are alive and fresh; opened shellfish are usually not.

Seafood will stay fresh for days when it is cured. The seasonings enter the meat, keeping it free from spoilage, preventing any 'fishy' smell, and spreading flavors through the meat.

Several recipes in this book require that seafood be served raw, but marinated in an acidic sauce. Certain acids cause seafood to go through chemical changes similar to those that take place during cooking. The marinated seafood will look and taste cooked, but will be even more tender.

When boiling seafood, it will be more flavorful if boiled in water that is almost as salty as the ocean (quite salty). If you use less salt, water will infuse into the seafood and dilute its flavor.

Shrimp, cooking:
Shrimp is done when the inside has just turned white and the outside pink. Overcooking will make it tough.

Simmer:
To simmer, bring a mixture to a boil, reduce the heat to low, and let the mixture bubble gently.

Terrine:
A terrine is an earthenware casserole dish.

Tomatoes - peeling and deseeding:
Gourmet chefs peel and deseed tomatoes mainly for aesthetics. You can prepare recipes without this step, but your dishes will be a little juicier (juice is removed when you deseed) and the skins will not dissolve into the sauce.

The technique is actually quite simple. Find the dot on the tomato's underside. Cut a skin deep "X" through the dot. Place the tomato in very hot water for 30 to 60 seconds. As soon as the cut skin begins to separate from the meat, place the tomato in ice cold water to prevent cooking. When cooled, peel the skin; it will slip right off.

To remove the seeds, cut the tomato in half from side to side (not top to bottom). Scoop the easily available seeds out with your finger, and flush any remaining seeds with water. The resulting tomato will be firm and meaty.

CONVERSIONS

3t = 1T

1 fluid oz. = 2T

8 fluid oz. = 1C

1 jigger = 1-1/2 oz. = 3T

2C = 1 pt.

2 pt. = 1 qt.

4 qt. = 1 gal.

16 oz. = 1 lb.

Butter 1/2C = 1 stick = 4 oz. = 8T

Cheese 1C = 2-1/2 to 3 oz.

Garlic 1 fresh clove = 1/8t powder

Herbs 1T fresh = 1/3 to 1/2T dried

Nuts 1C = 5 to 6 oz.

INGREDIENT SUBSTITUTIONS

INGREDIENT	DESCRIPTION	SUBSTITUTION
Albuquerque Chili Powder	A light red chili powder, easily found in the southwest.	Use a little less cayenne.
Anaheim Chile	A mildly hot, common green chili.	Any mildly hot green chili.
Ancho Powder	Hot pepper powder, not as hot as cayenne.	Any hot red chili powder.
Arugula	Leafy green herb used in salads. Radishy taste.	Romaine lettuce or watercress.
Baquette	A long, thin loaf of French bread.	Italian bread
Blue Corn	A variety of corn grown in the southwest.	Yellow corn
Canola Oil	A low fat vegetable oil.	Any vegetable oil.
Chardonnay	Dry, white wine	Any dry, white wine.
Chayote	Light green southwestern squash, shaped like a pear.	Zucchini cooked al dente.
Chervil	An aromatic herb of the carrot family. More delicate flavor and form than parsley.	When used as a garnish, you can substitute parsley.
Chipotle	Smoked and dried Jalapeños. Can be purchased as paste or powder. Jalapeños turn dark red and become very hot when smoked.	Very hot red chile paste or powder.
Chorizo	Mexican or Spanish pork sausage. Highly seasoned with cayenne, pimentos, garlic, and paprika.	No good substitute.
Cilantro	Coriander leaves. Unique zesty flavor.	There is no good substitute for cilantro. Fresh cilantro is much more flavorful than dried.

INGREDIENT	DESCRIPTION	SUBSTITUTION
Clarified Butter	Butter that has been cooked and separated. Only the fatty part of the butter that is less likely to burn is used.	To make your own, melt butter (do not boil or stir). The whey will settle to the bottom; do not use it. Ladle the top layer and store it in the refrigerator. It will keep for months. Regular butter may be used, but you must cook slowly to prevent burning.
Clarified Chicken Stock	Chicken stock, strained and fat skimmed off.	Make your own.
Cointreau	Orange -flavored liqueur	Easily available.
Filo	Paper thin sheets of dough.	Available in frozen food section of most stores.
Frangelico	Hazelnut liqueur	Amaretto
Frisee	A delicate lettuce, usually picked young.	Any delicate lettuce.
Juniper Berries	Aromatic berries of the juniper tree.	Available in the herb section of natural food stores. No good substitute.
Kosher Salt	A salt coarser than table salt.	Use 1/4 less table salt.
Maggi Seasoning	Found in Oriental markets and some grocers.	No good substitute.
Puff Pastry	A light, flaky pastry that puffs greatly when baked.	Easily available frozen.
Radicchio	A slightly bitter Italian red lettuce with white veins. Grows in round heads.	Belgian Endive
Sauce Demi Glaze	Stock reduced to great thickness. Can be purchased at gourmet stores.	Add roux to thicken the drippings of any meat.
Scallion	Green onion, mild flavor.	Easily available.

INGREDIENT	DESCRIPTION	SUBSTITUTION
Shallot	Hot onion, with a slight taste of garlic.	Easily available.
Shiitake mushrooms	Large, chewy, brown Oriental mushroom.	Found in most grocery stores, fresh or dried.
Sonoran Seasoning	A blend of herbs and spices developed by Chef Alan Zeman. Used as an all purpose seasoning, is especially aromatic on grilled seafood, poultry and meats.	Can be ordered from Alan Zeman's Southwestern Originals (see Mail Order Appendix). Or substitute salt or Mexican seasoning.
Tomato Concasse	Pureed and strained tomatoes reduced to a thick consistency.	Tomato puree
Tomato Coulis	Peeled, deseeded, and pureed tomatoes.	Puree peeled and deseeded tomatoes.
Unsalted Butter	Many chefs prefer to use unsalted butter, then salt to taste.	Use regular butter and less salt.

MAIL ORDER SOURCES
FOR SOUTHWEST INGREDIENTS

Cahill Desert Products
490 East Pima Street
Phoenix, AZ 85004
(602) 956-2030

Prickly pear products, chilies, cactus jellies and candies, jalapeño honey mustard, syrups, etc.

Chef Alan Zeman's Southwestern Originals
P.O. Box 31283
Tucson, AZ 85712
(602) 296-0398

The only source for Mr. Zeman's original Sonoran Seasonings and Prickly Pear Barbeque Glaze.

Josie's Best
P.O. Box 5525
Santa Fe, NM 85701
(505) 983-6520

Tortillas, green and red chile, posole, blue corn, fry bread, sopaipilla mix, etc. Fresh and dried products.

K. Benson Company
3400 South Mill Avenue, Number 25
Tempe, AZ 85282
(602) 966-0272

Full range of Southwest and gourmet specialty foods, cooking supplies, and gifts.

Mount Hope
104 Main Street
Cottonwood, AZ 86326
(602) 634-8251

Large selection of natural foods and herbs, including juniper berries.

Peppers, Inc.
4009 North Brown Avenue
Scottsdale, AZ 85251
(800) 999-0217

Almost anything to do with chilies: ristras, salsas, ceramics, Christmas lights, etc.

Territorial Gourmet Foods, Inc.
2766 North Country Club Road
Tucson, AZ 85716
(602) 323-3322

Salsa, condiments, prepared dried Southwestern meals, chilies, etc.

INDEX

NOTES